ABANDONED COLORADO

A HISTORY TOLD IN RUINS

EVAN J. ALDERSON

AMERICA
THROUGH
TIME

America Through Time is an imprint of Sutton Publishing Inc
www.through-time.com
office@through-time.com

First published 2021
Reprinted 2025

ISBN 978-1-63499-369-2

Typeset in Trade Gothic 10pt on 15pt
Printed and bound in England

CONTENTS

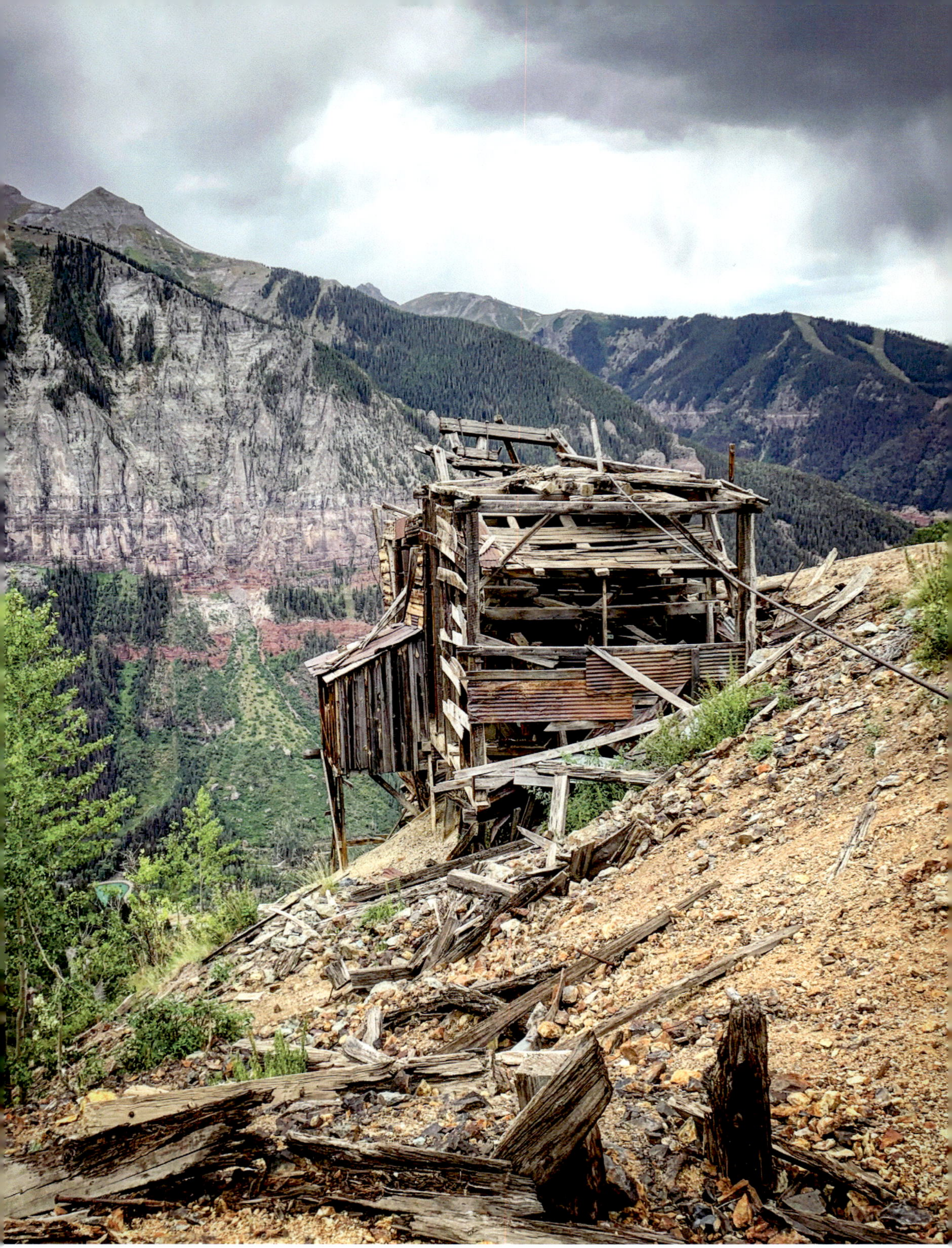

Little about this crumbling ruin at the Smuggler-Union mine suggests the pivotal role it played in Colorado's history.

INTRODUCTION

High atop a desolate peak, a weather-beaten shack clings to the mountain as it has for 100 years. There are no interpretive signs, no tour guides—nothing to tell of the fortunes made here, the battles fought, or the lives lost. It is a forgotten piece of Colorado's history—one of thousands, scattered across the Great Plains and tucked in every corner of the Rocky Mountains. These ruins stood silent witness to the tempestuous and often violent birth of a state. They are the unmarked monuments to great ambition, great success, and inevitable doom. In these pages, I have sought to capture and record the story of these bygone places before they are consigned to oblivion.

1

THE PIKES PEAK GOLD RUSH

Before the mid-nineteenth century, Colorado was a nameless place through which folks passed on their way to somewhere else. During the California Gold Rush, however, as prospectors traveled west across the Great Plains, rumors began to circulate of gold in the creeks that ran down from the uncharted Rockies. In 1858, William "Green" Russell, a Georgian prospector, led a group of 108 men to the site of present-day Denver. There, at the mouth of Little Dry Creek, they pulled up 20 ounces of gold.

The discovery kicked off what became known as the Pikes Peak Gold Rush—Pikes Peak was actually nowhere near the mining scene, but the snow-capped mountain became a prominent landmark to those who crossed the Great Plains. Some 100,000 people immigrated to the region within just three years. The name given to this massive influx of prospectors was the "Fifty-Niners." Their famed motto was "Pikes Peak or Bust."

Many of the miners that came had already tried their hand in the California Gold Rush. The veterans among them began searching upstream for source veins. In January 1859, a daring prospector by the name of George Andrew Jackson trudged into the snow-covered Rocky Mountains, discovering gold deposits near some natural hot springs. The area rapidly developed into the highly successful Idaho Springs Mining District. At the same time, a group camped at present-day Boulder found rich placers on Gold Hill.

In May of the same year, John H. Gregory discovered a rich, gold lode deposit just north of Idaho Springs (then referred to as "Jackson's Diggings"). It was the first hardrock vein to be discovered in Colorado. News of the find spread quickly, drawing in 10,000 men by month's end. The region was touted as the "Richest Square Mile on Earth."

Within the year, several towns had formed in support of the new mines. Black Hawk and Central City (then called Mountain City) were two of these settlements that have survived to the present. Lesser known and since abandoned was the nearby town of Nevadaville. Originally called Nevada City, the modest municipality consisted of a general store, several saloons, a church, and a town hall that doubled as the fire station and a Masonic temple that, strangely, still holds meetings to this day.

As summer approached and the snow melted, many prospectors began venturing deeper into the Rockies. Placer deposits were soon discovered along Blue River, in South Park, and in California Gulch. At Blue River, the now-famous ski town of Breckenridge (then spelled "Breckinridge" in honor of the vice president) was formed. Dozens of small mining settlements sprang up all around South Park. Most notable among these were Tarryall, Fairplay, Buckskin Joe, Sterling, and Montgomery. All but Fairplay have since been abandoned. The town of Montgomery is now submerged beneath Montgomery Reservoir.

Rich placer gold was also found in California Gulch where a mining camp called Oro City was formed. Miners here were plagued by strange black sand that collected in their sluice boxes. It was not until fourteen years later that the substance was identified as the lead mineral cerussite. This would eventually lead to the founding and naming of Leadville, but more on that later.

Shortly after becoming a U.S. territory in 1861, Colorado experienced a massive population decline. The civil war had begun, and many men returned to their home state to enlist. Additionally, the easily mined surface gold had been largely exploited and many of the alpine boom towns were left abandoned. The Pike's Peak Gold Rush was over and the young territory slipped slowly into the doldrums.

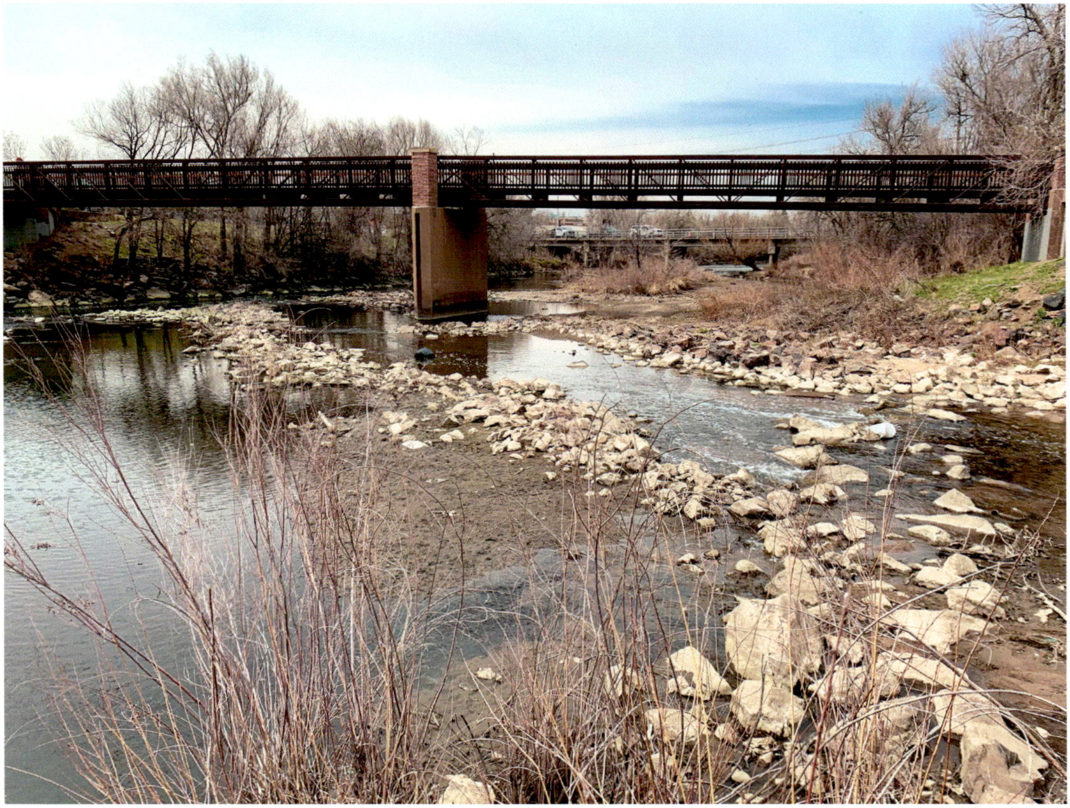

Above: The confluence of Little Dry Creek and the Platte River where the William Green Russel party discovered gold.

Right: A gated adit near Gold Hill. Though lesser known than Idaho Springs or Central City, Gold Hill was one of the earliest and most profitable gold-producing districts in Colorado.

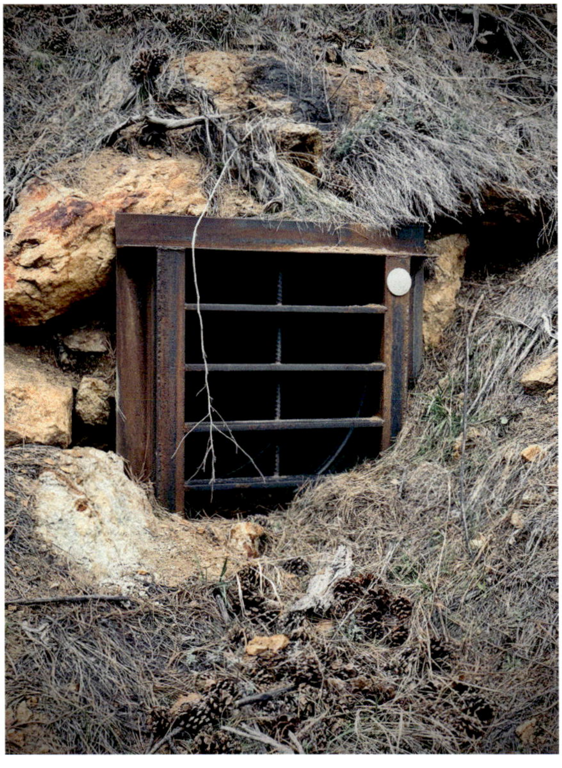

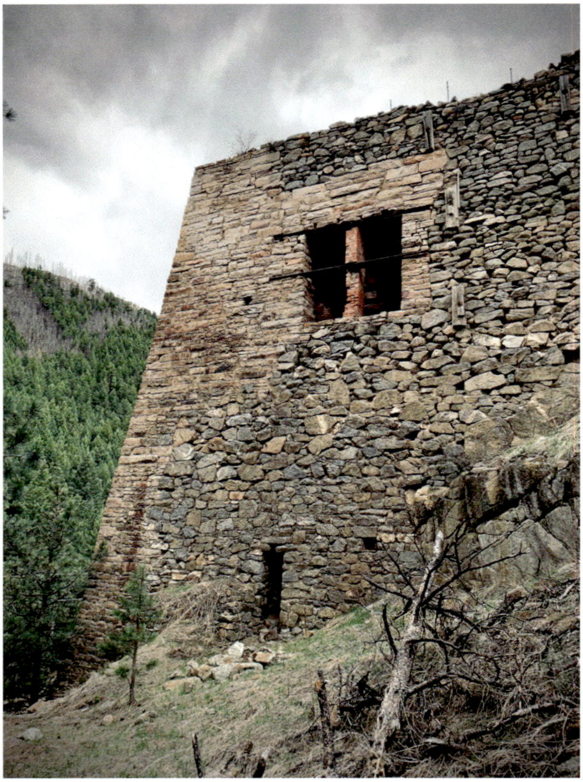

Ruins of the enormous Wall Street Mill. The town of Wall Street replaced an early mining camp known as Delphi, which was within the Nebraska Territory before Colorado became its own state.

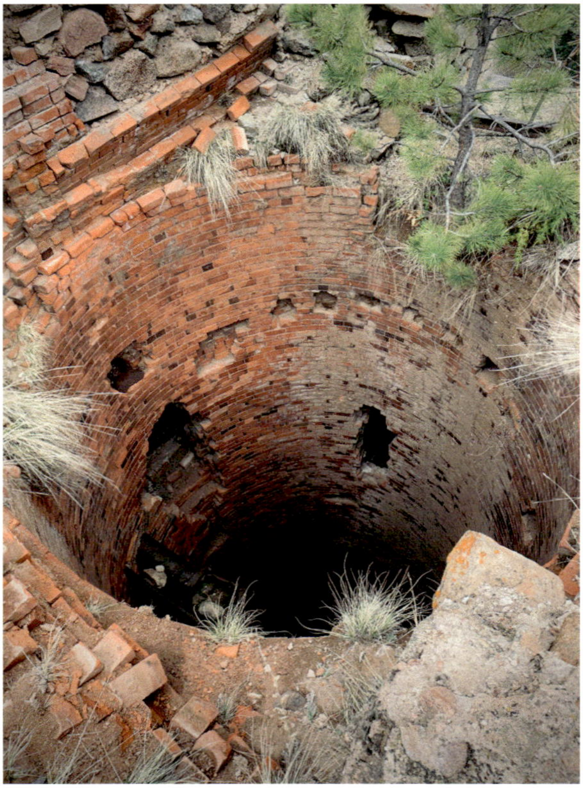

The Wall Street Mill was one of the first chlorination mills in the state and cost $150,000 to build in 1902. This 50-foot tower was used to cool ore after the roasting process.

Opposite above: The Stanley mine in Idaho Springs sits along Clear Creek, where George Andrew Jackson discovered gold in 1859.

Opposite below: An ore cart, once belonging to the Storm King mine, sits outside an old assay office west of Salina.

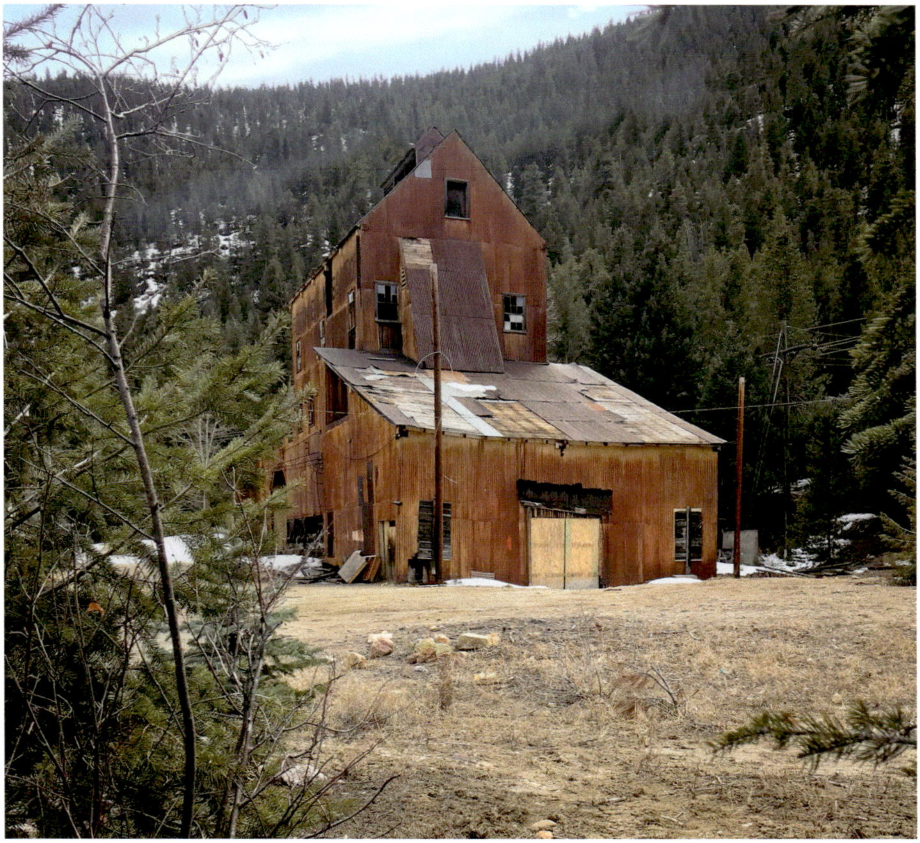

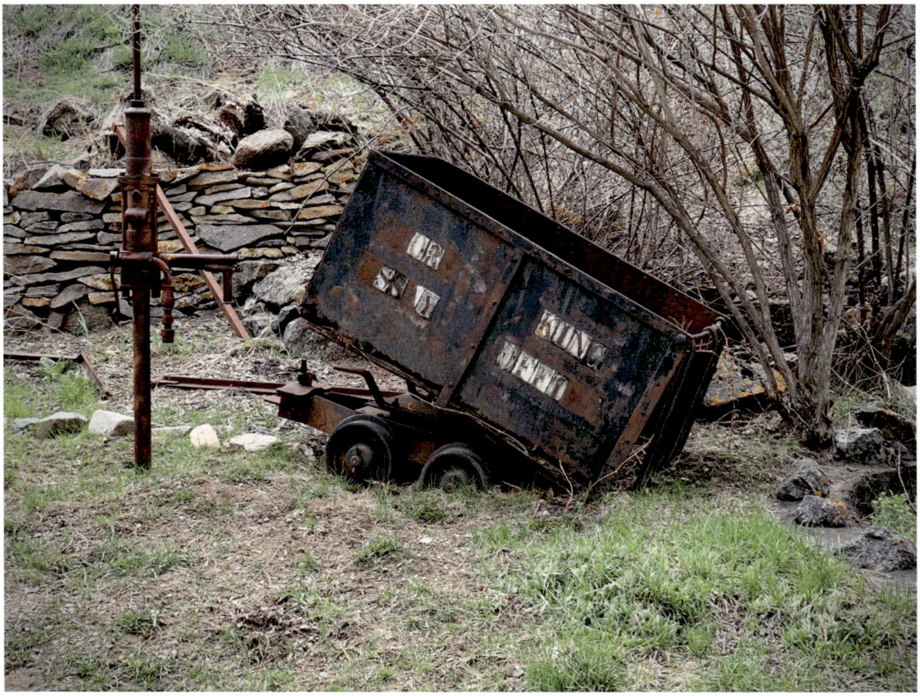
KING

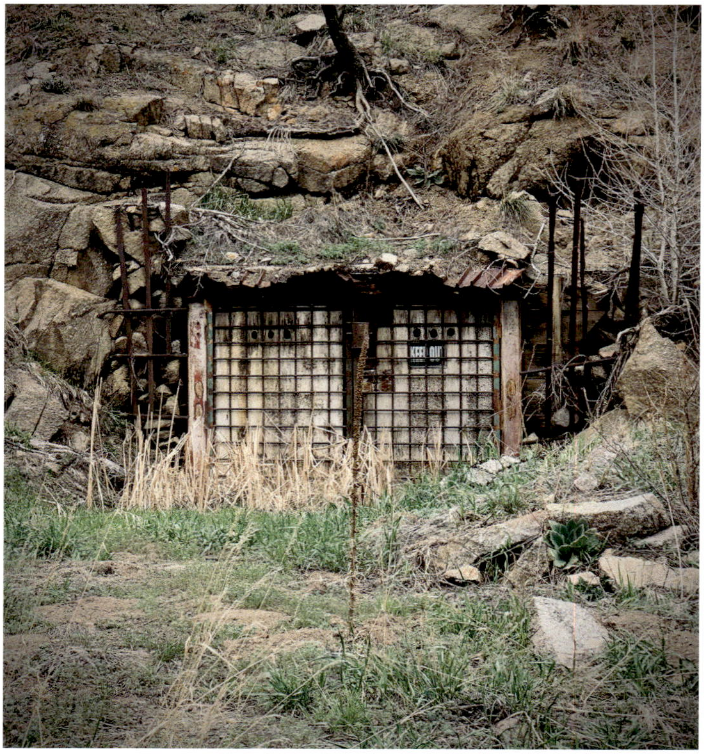

Left: The Wood mine along Fourmile Creek. Though just 1 mile or so from Gold Hill, gold was not discovered here until 1891. This mine was the last to close in the district.

Below: The Coeur d'Alene mine shaft house stands atop a hill, overlooking Central City.

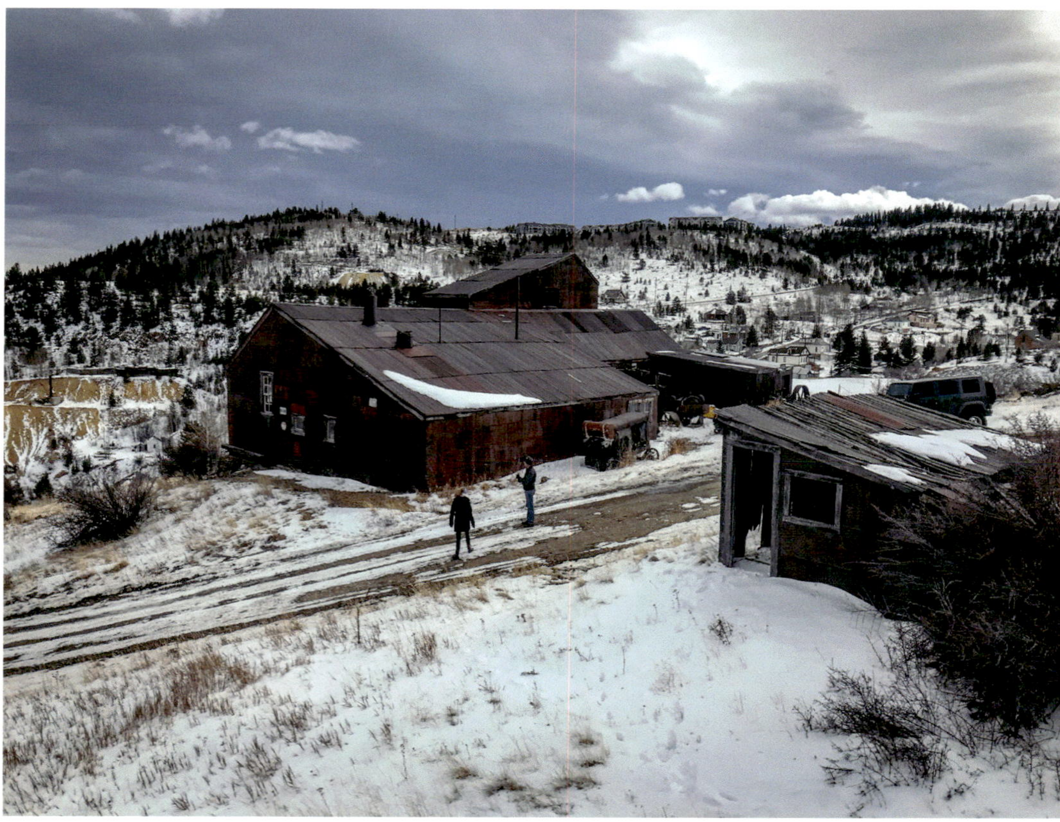

The Stanley Vein mine is an abandoned fluorite mine in Jamestown, very near where the first gold discovery was made in Boulder County (then the Nebraska Territory).

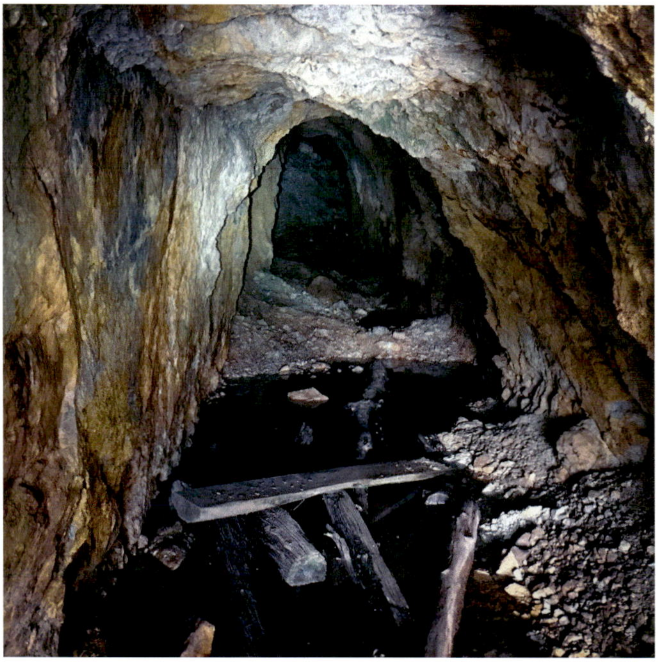

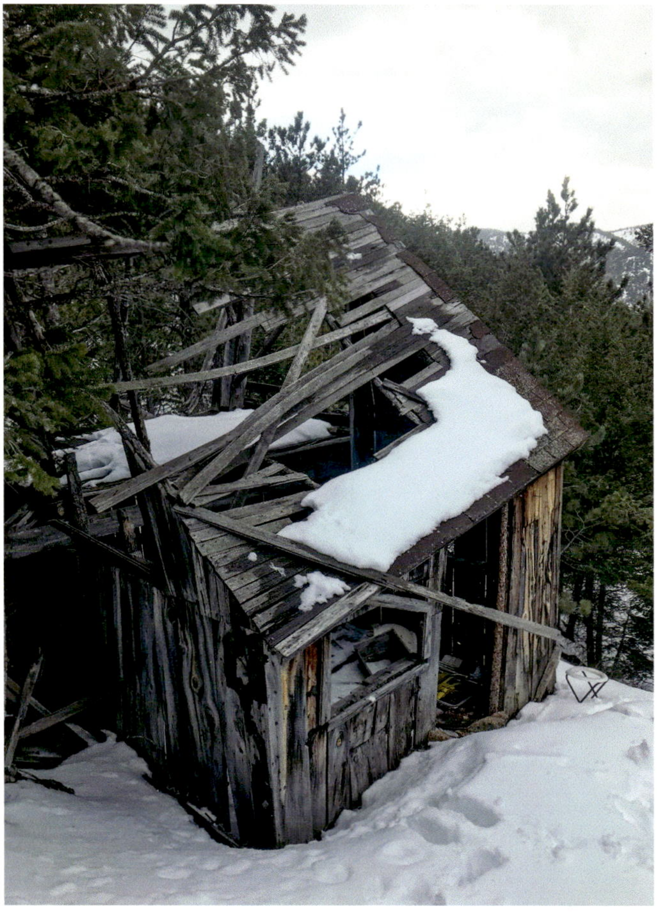

An old miner's shack at the Maud S mine.

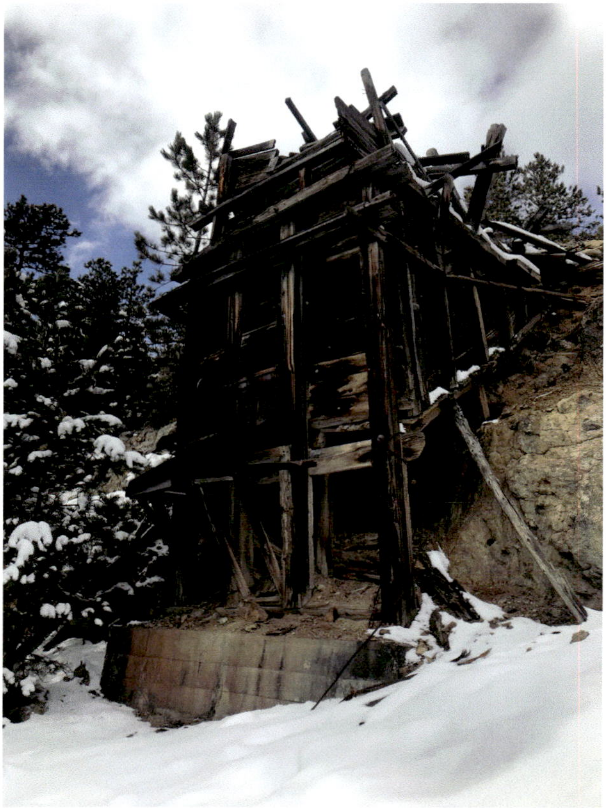

Left: A wood ore hopper at the Emmit mine, outside Jamestown.

Below: The Pozo mine shaft house stands just south of Nevadaville in an area once teeming with prospectors.

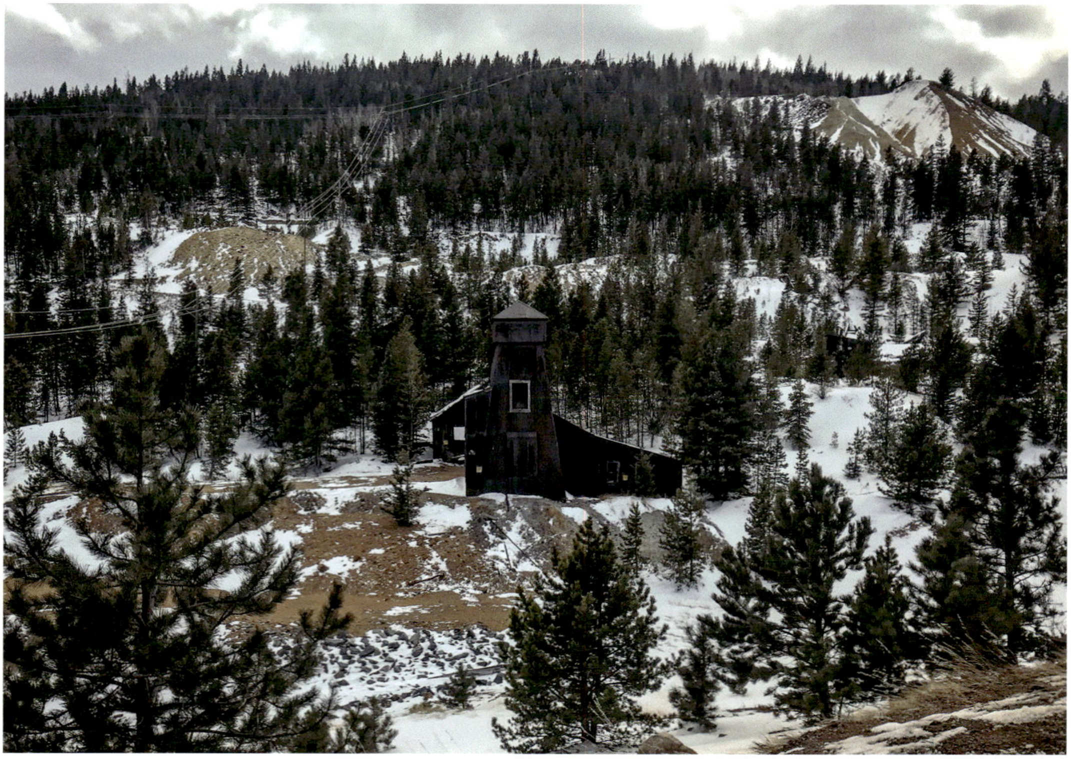

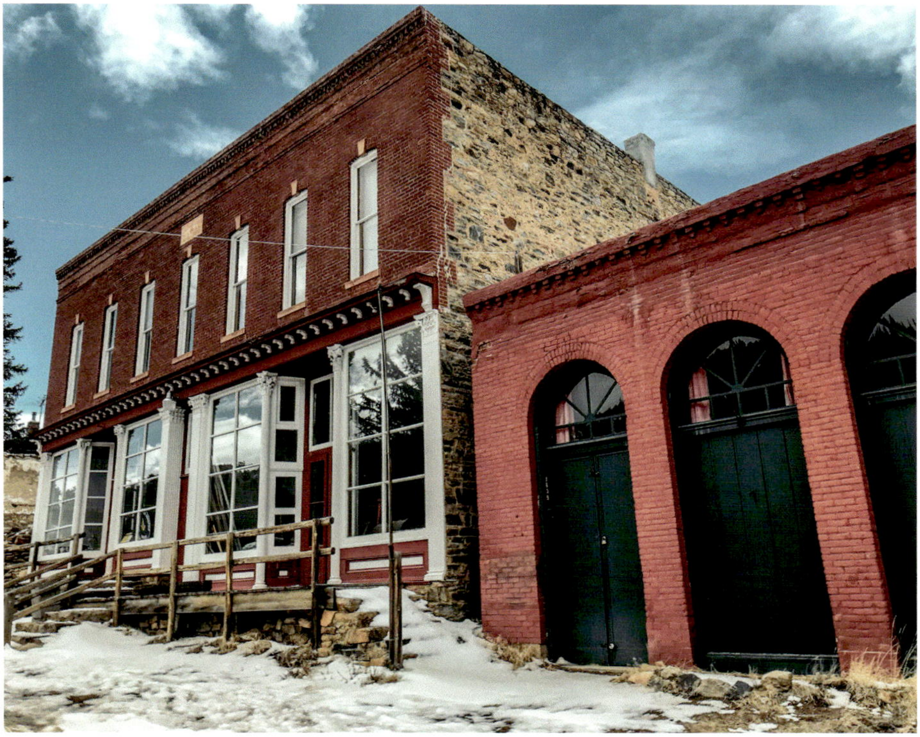

Standing structures in present-day Nevadaville. The building on the left is the Masonic Temple, which still holds meetings.

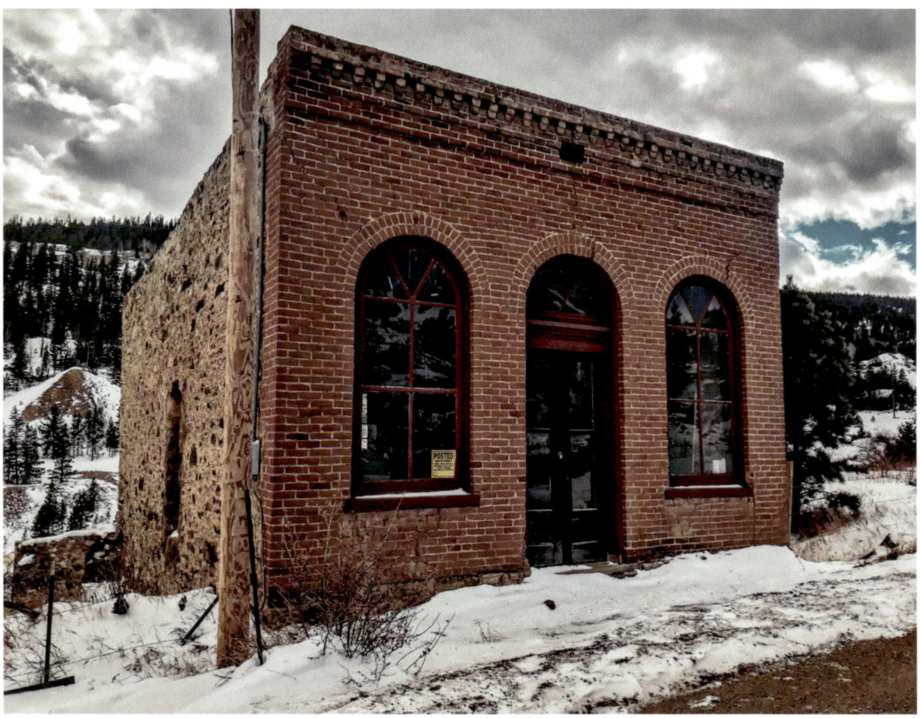

The Bon Ton Saloon was abandoned along with the rest of Nevadaville in the 1930s.

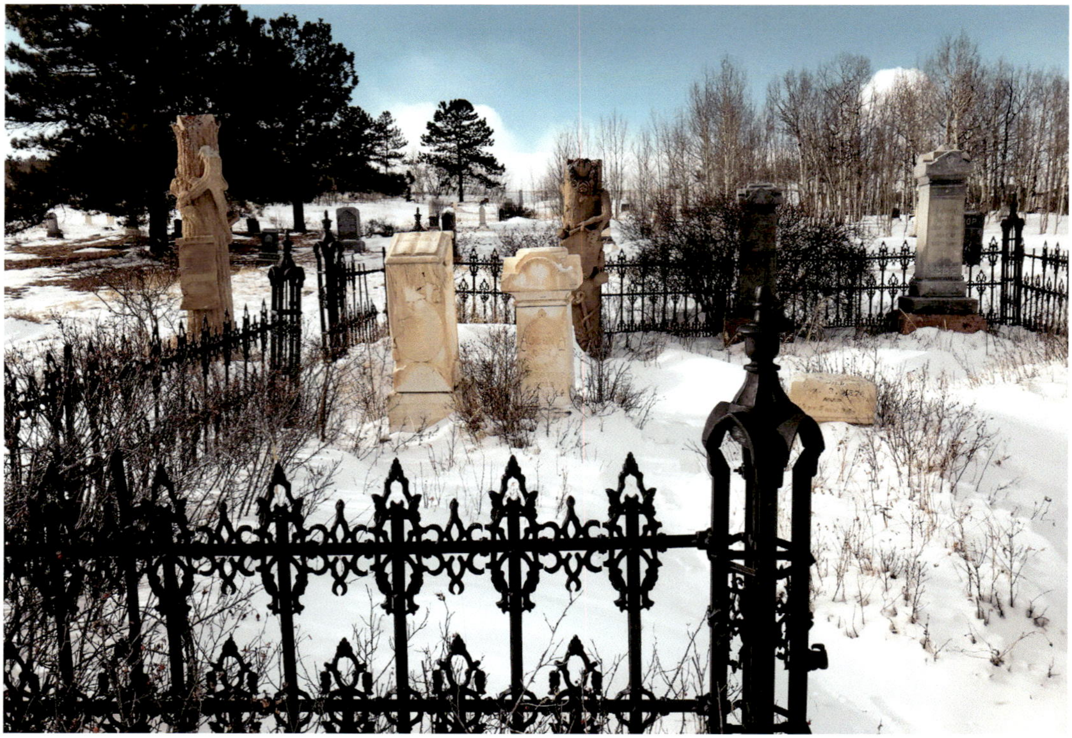

Headstones at the Rocky Mountain Independent Order of Oddfellows Cemetery, outside Central City.

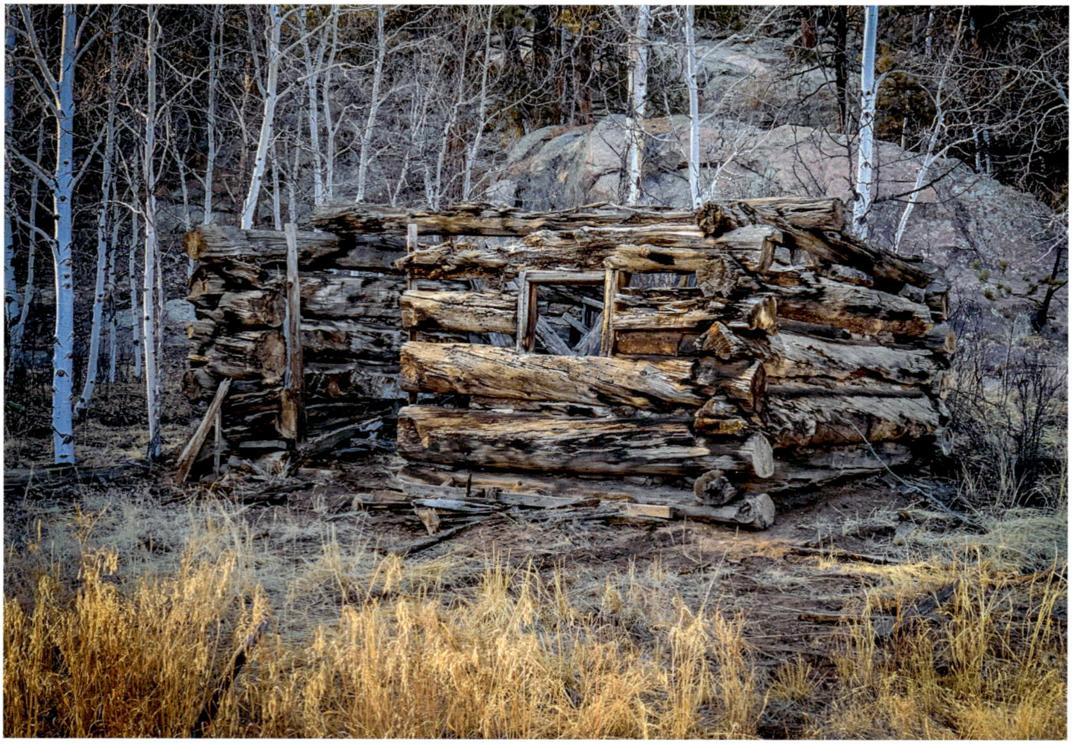

Primitive miners' cabins like this one can be found all over South Park.

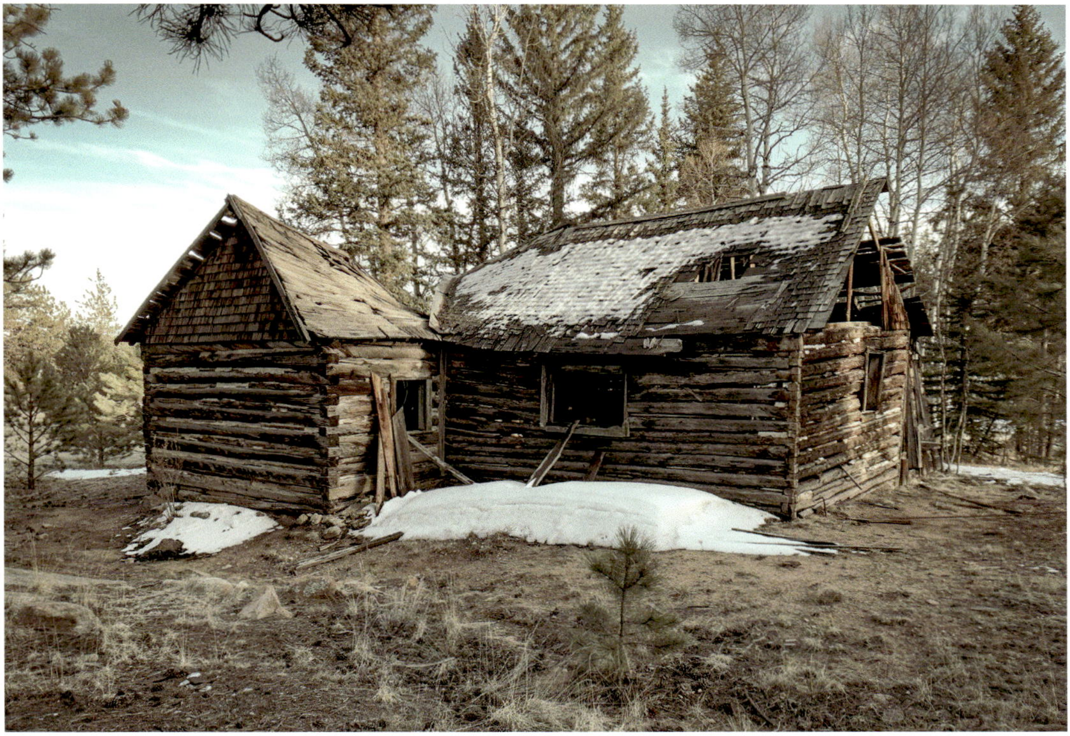

The largest standing structure in a small, unnamed settlement near Tarryall.

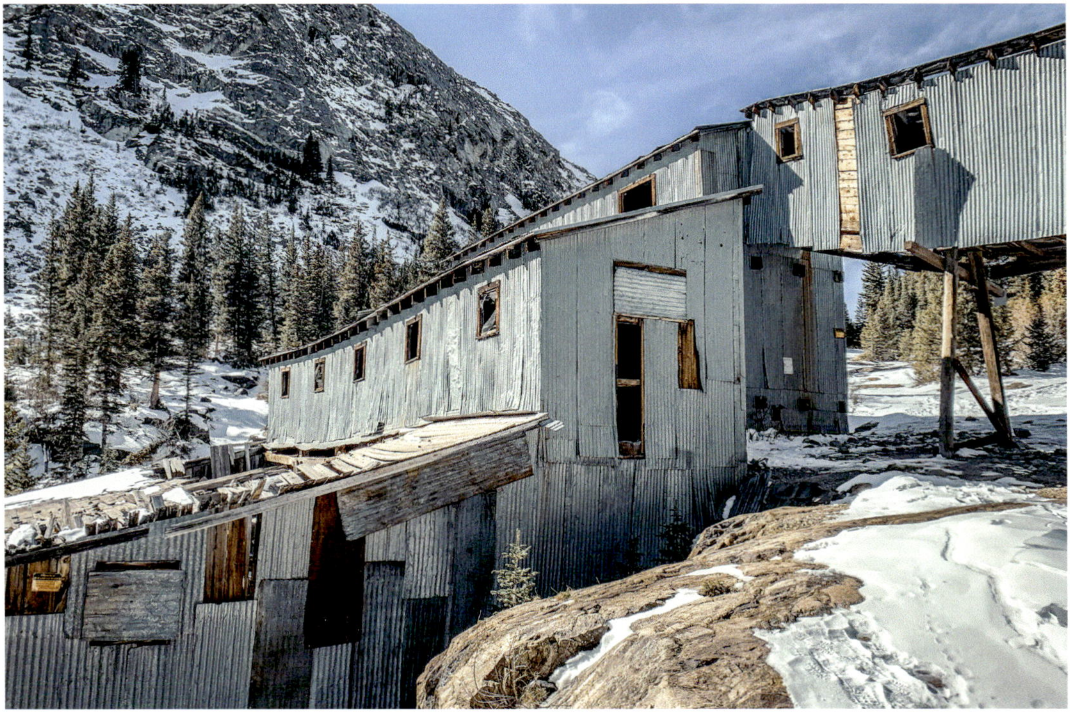

The Magnolia Mill is all that is left of the town of Montgomery, which was flooded in 1890 to create a reservoir for the city of Colorado Springs.

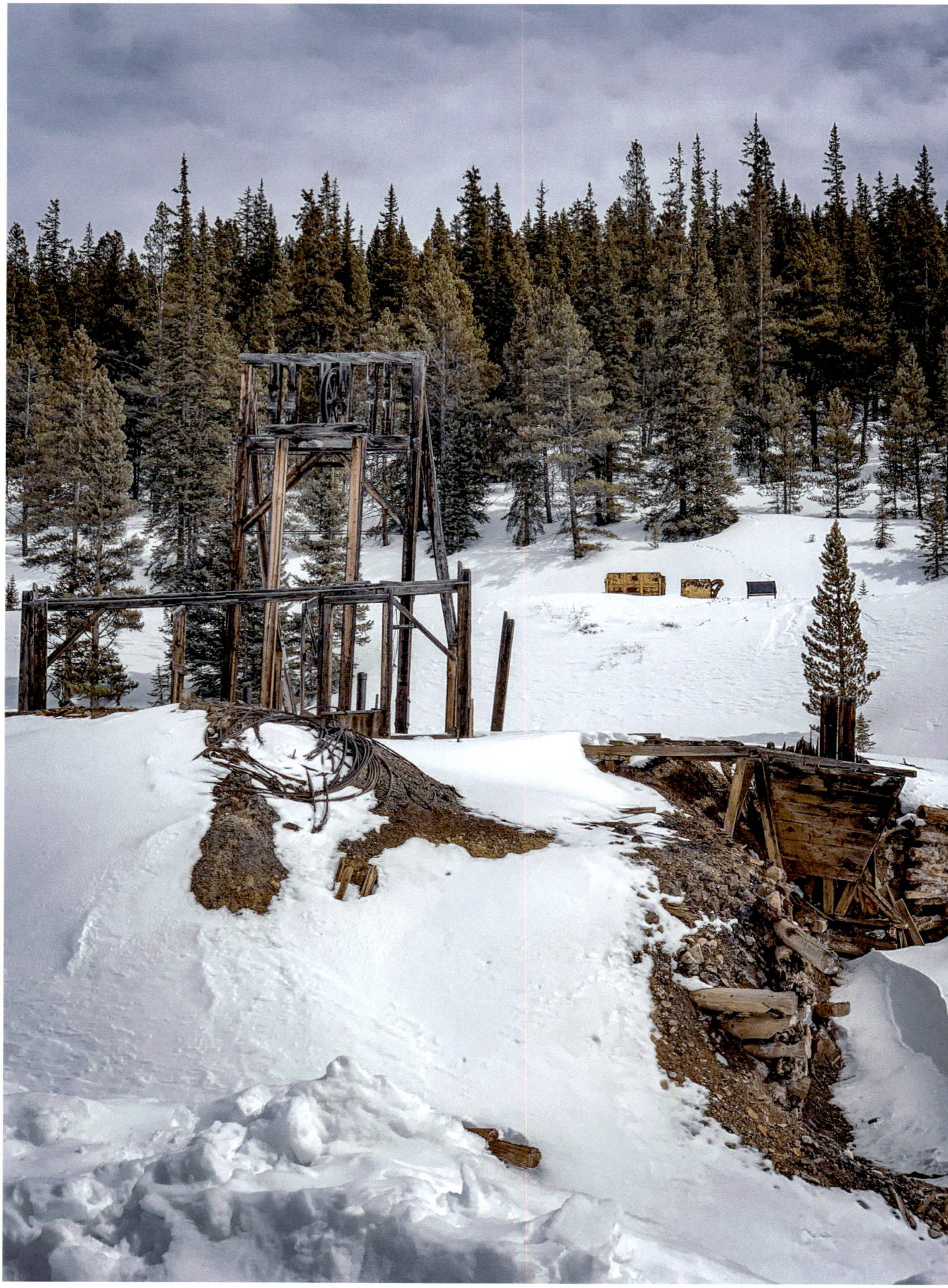

California Gulch, the site of Oro City, later became the scene of extensive lead and silver mining. This decaying headframe marks the bygone settlement's approximate location.

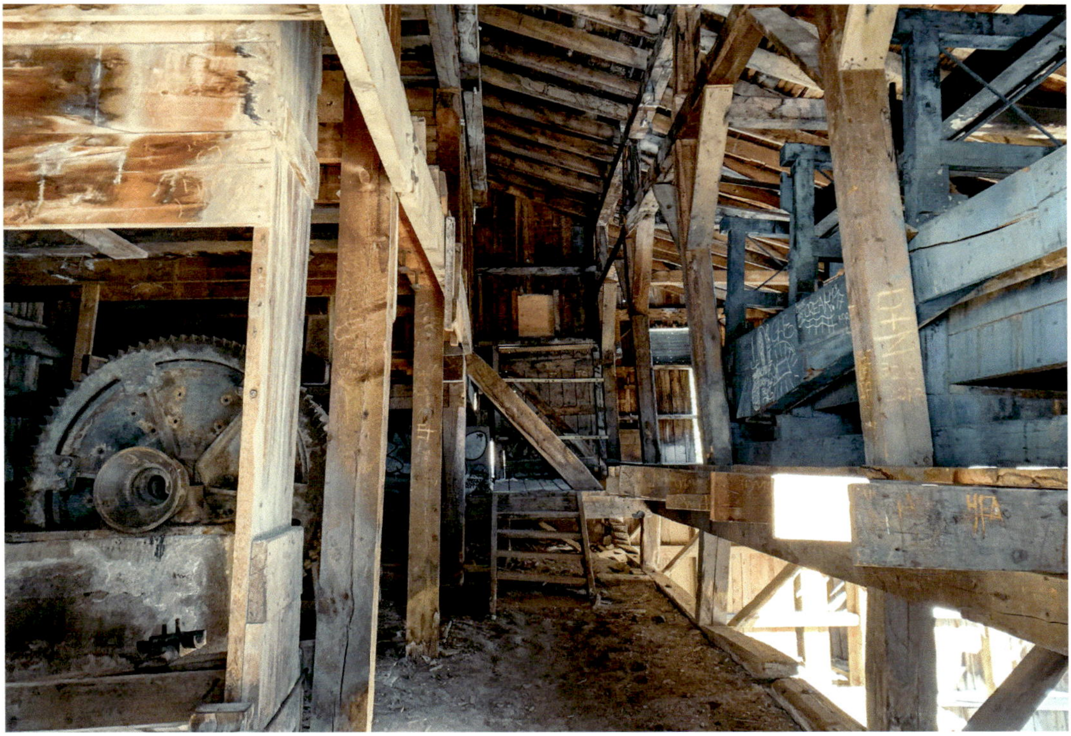

Inside the Magnolia Mill. The structure was built in 1930 to replace the original, which burned in a fire.

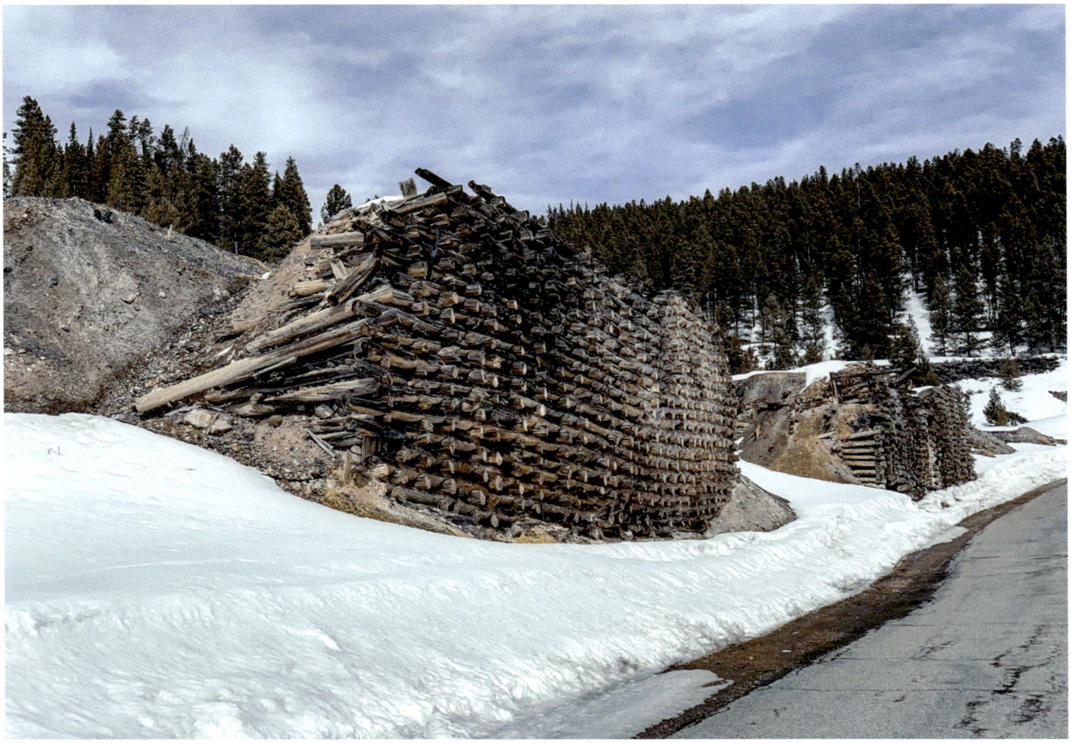

Cribbing at the Greenbacks mine in California Gulch. This was once a railroad crossover point.

2

THE GILDED AGE

For the miners that stayed, the race was still on to find the source veins. Following the suspected path of the Colorado Mineral Belt, many prospectors ventured southwest, discovering lode deposits along the Mosquito Range, near present-day Alma and Leadville.

In 1878, a Breckenridge-based prospector named Harry Farncomb discovered the source of the French Gulch placer gold. While digging around on a shale-covered hill near the small town of Lincoln City, Farncomb uncovered a decaying quartz vein, laced with ribbons of gold. He called his discovery the "Wire Patch" for the strange way the metal occurred in the rock.

Rather than stake a claim, which would have tipped off his competition, Farncomb spent the next two years quietly buying up all the nearby land until he owned the entire hill. In 1880, he walked into a Denver bank and deposited 300 troy ounces of gold. As Farncomb anticipated, a profusion of prying prospectors promptly descended on his hill. Discovering the entire area to be private property, many were outraged, accusing Farncomb of cheating. A lengthy legal battle ensued, ultimately culminating into an all-out gunfight on the hill involving forty men. Three lost their lives, and many more were wounded. Farncomb eventually sold his holdings, retiring a rich man.

Breckenridge gained further notoriety when a miner named Tom Groves discovered a massive chunk of solid gold, weighing 13.2 pounds. The nugget was the largest piece of gold ever found in Colorado. Swaddling the ore in burlap, Groves ran back to Breckinridge where he paraded it through the streets, cradling the nugget like an infant. The gold piece became affectionately known as "Tom's Baby." It has since gone missing.

Unlike the early days of sifting gold out of stream beds, hard rock mining required immense infrastructure. Heavy machinery and explosives had to be hauled in, headframes erected, and mills and smelters built to crush and process the raw ore. Though constructing such facilities was no easy task, transporting materials over the mountainous terrain proved to be the greatest challenge.

Early freight lines relied on mules and wagons with severely limited payloads. The introduction of alpine railroads was a major boost to the mines and towns of the Rockies. The price of shipping goods and ore plummeted. Subsequently, wages dropped, businesses boomed, and lower-grade mining opportunities suddenly became economically feasible.

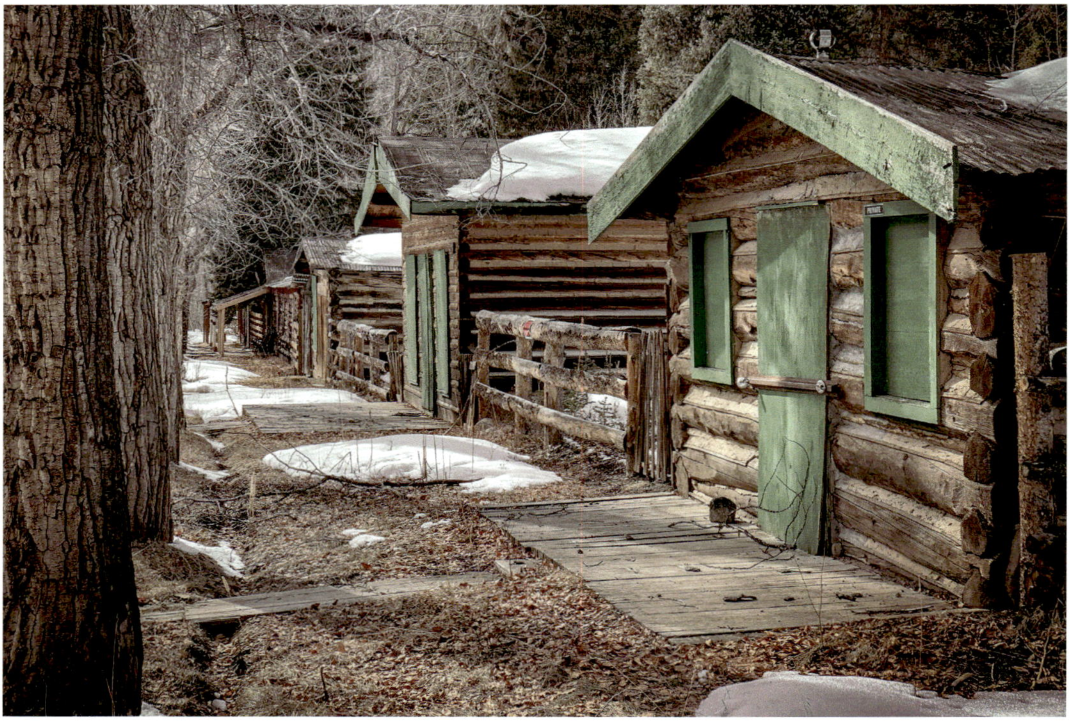

Float gold was discovered in Clear Creek in 1867, giving birth to several small, mining settlements, including the (mostly abandoned) town of Vicksburg, seen here.

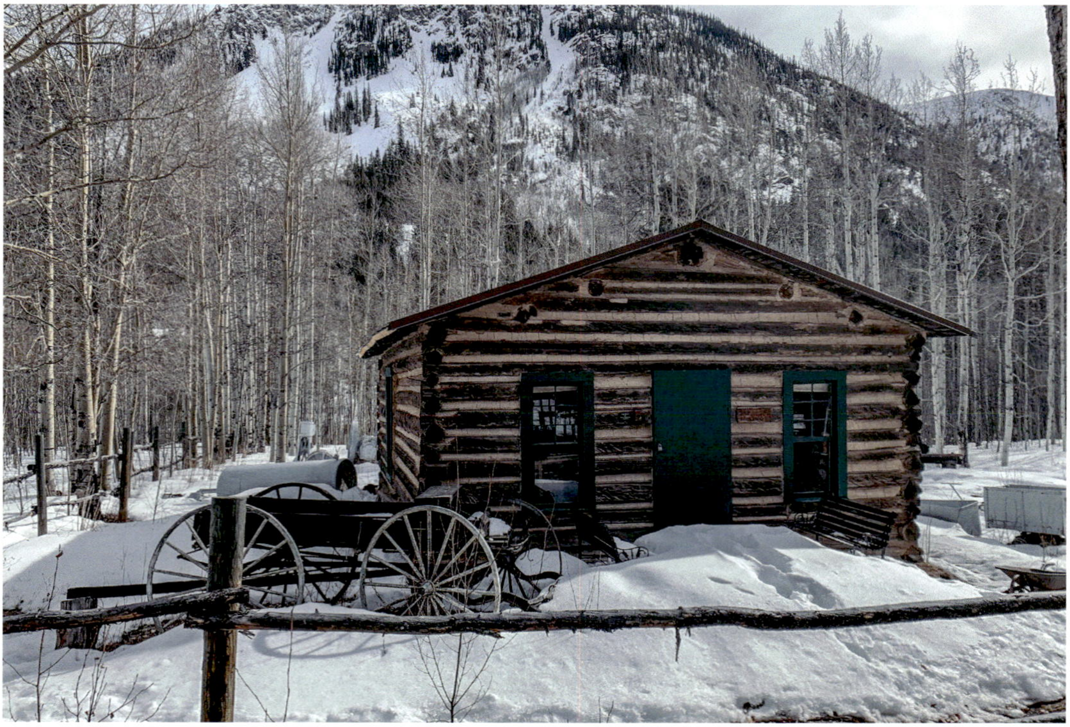

This log cabin has been repurposed as a modest museum, operated by a historical society during the summer months.

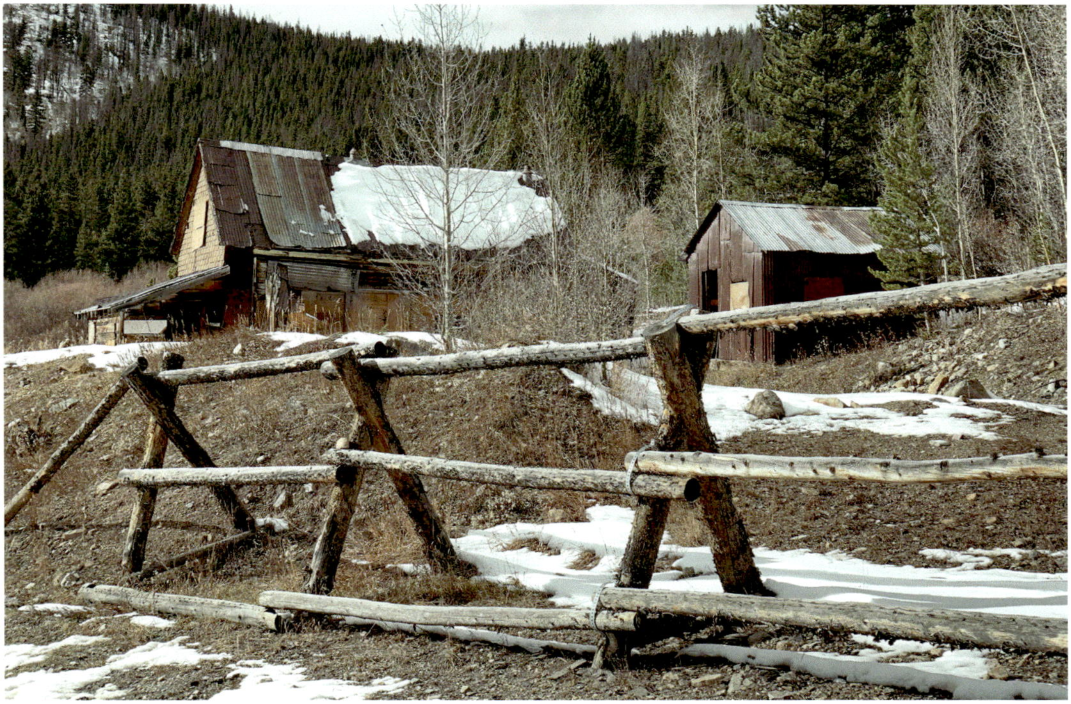

A handful of structures still stand at the ghost town of Lincolnville. It was here that Henry Farncomb discovered his famous Wire Patch mine.

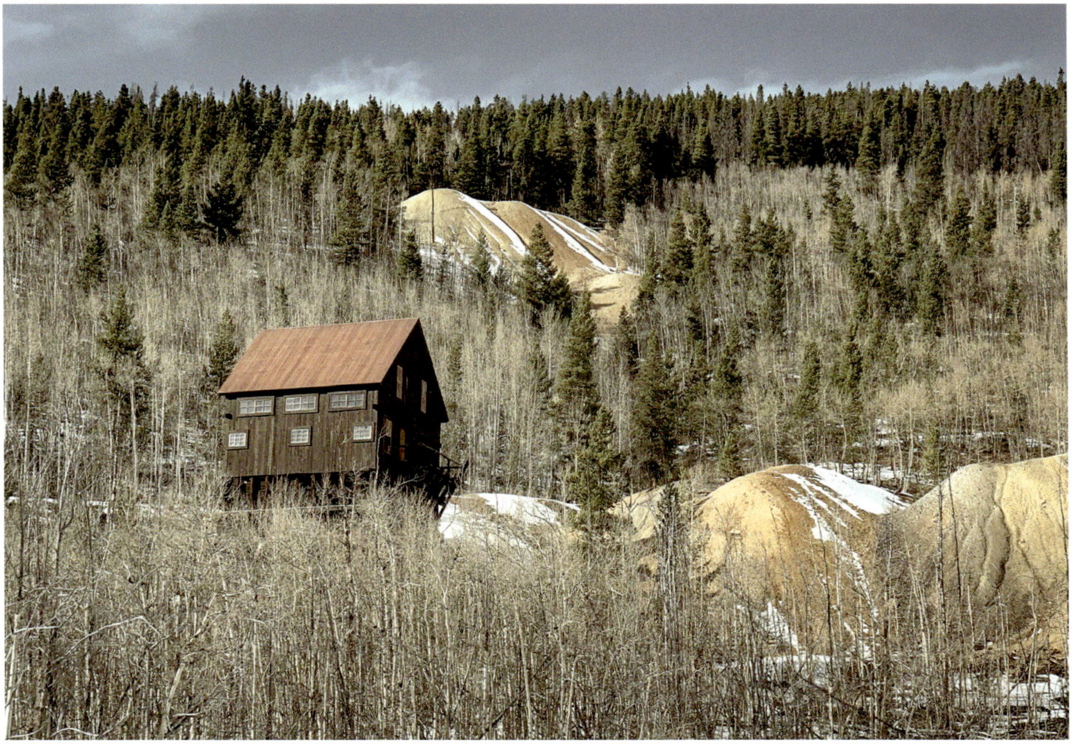

Orehouse at the Extenuate mine, in French Gulch.

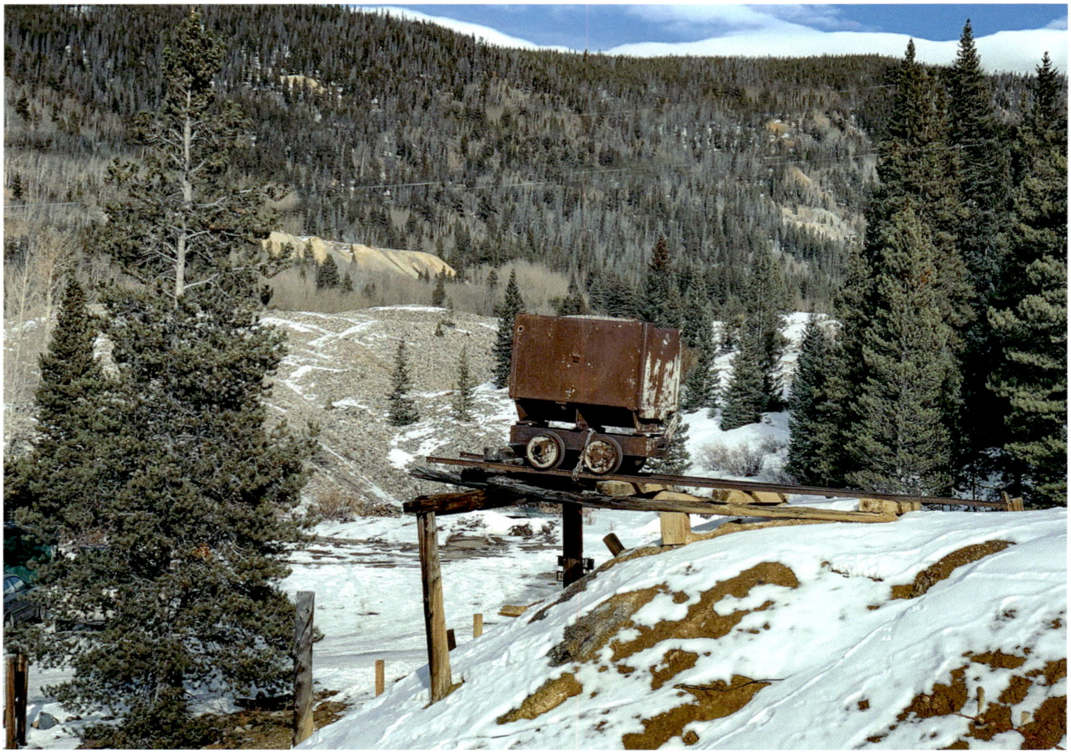

An ore cart perched atop a dump pile in French Gulch.

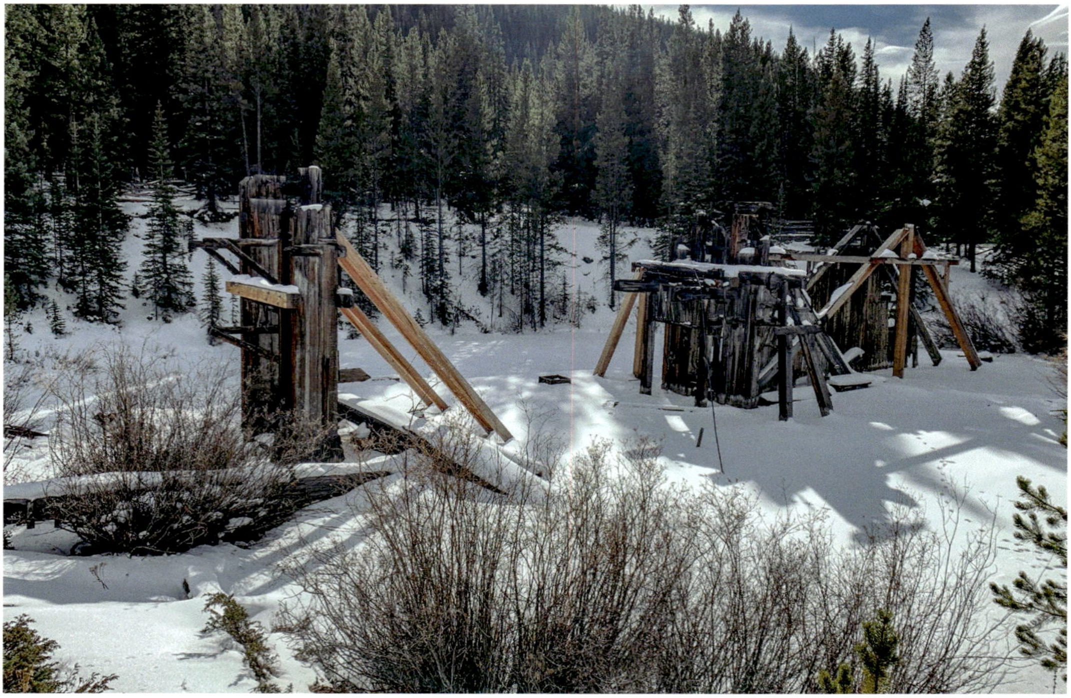

Beginning in 1898, huge dredges like the Reiling Dredge, shown here, were used to scour the riverbeds for the last traces of placer gold in French Gulch.

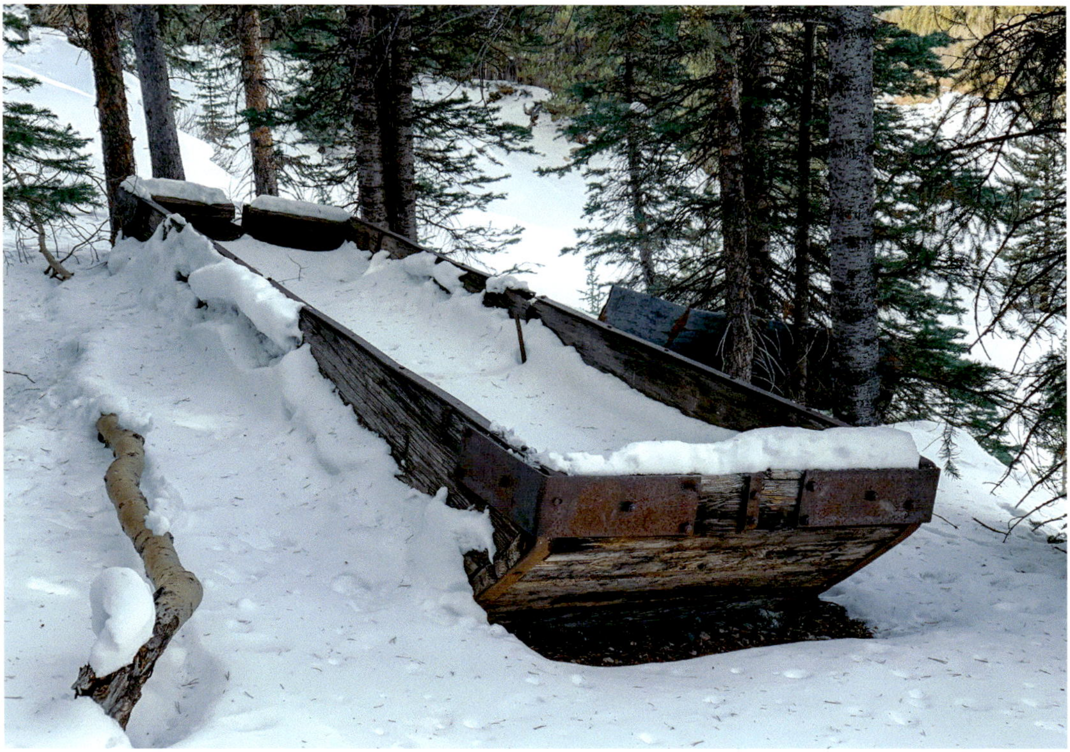

This may have been a skiff, which was used to move men and material between the dredge and shore.

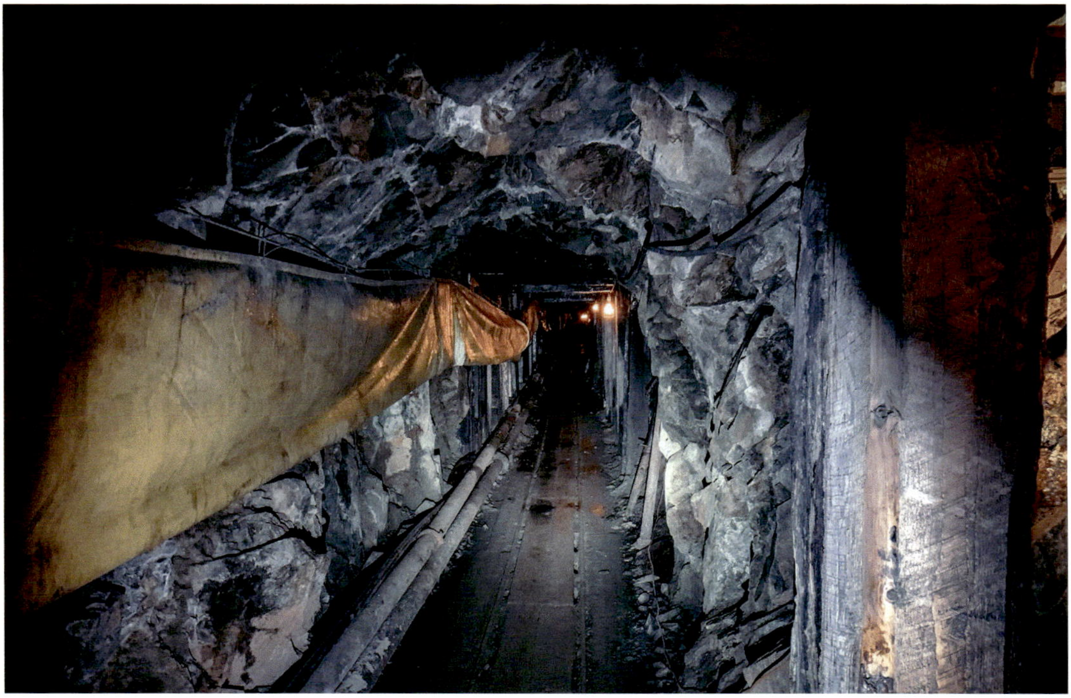

Farncomb's Wire Patch mine was the first of hundreds that sprang up near Breckenridge. Shown here is the Country Boy mine, which began operations in 1887.

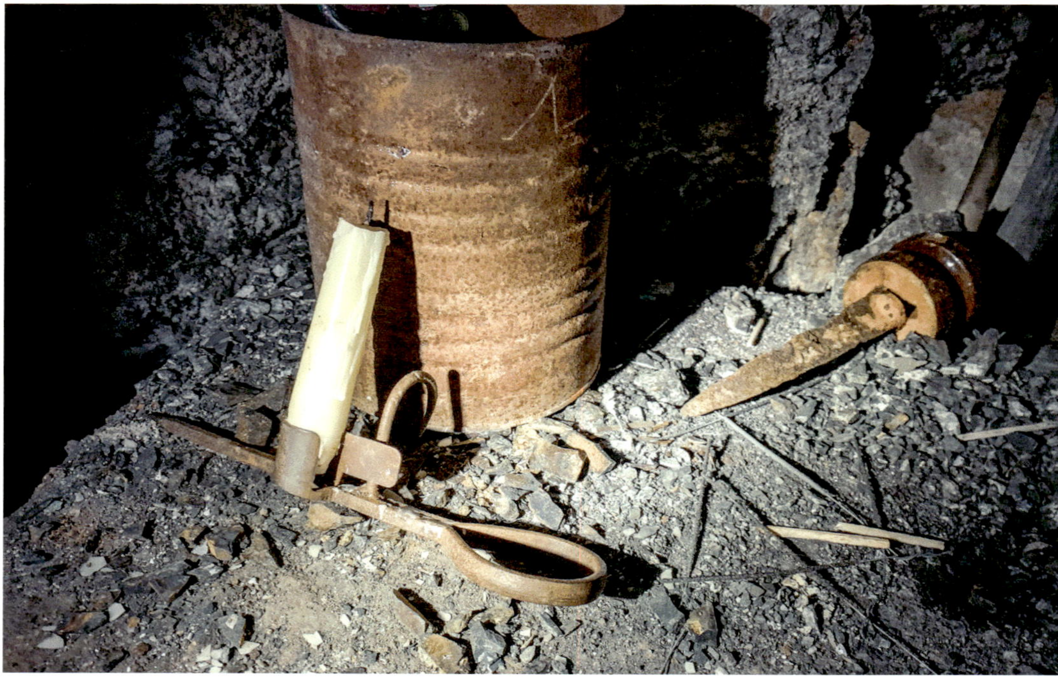

In the early lode mining days, work was done by candlelight, using "sticking tommys" like this one I found in a mine near Lincolnville.

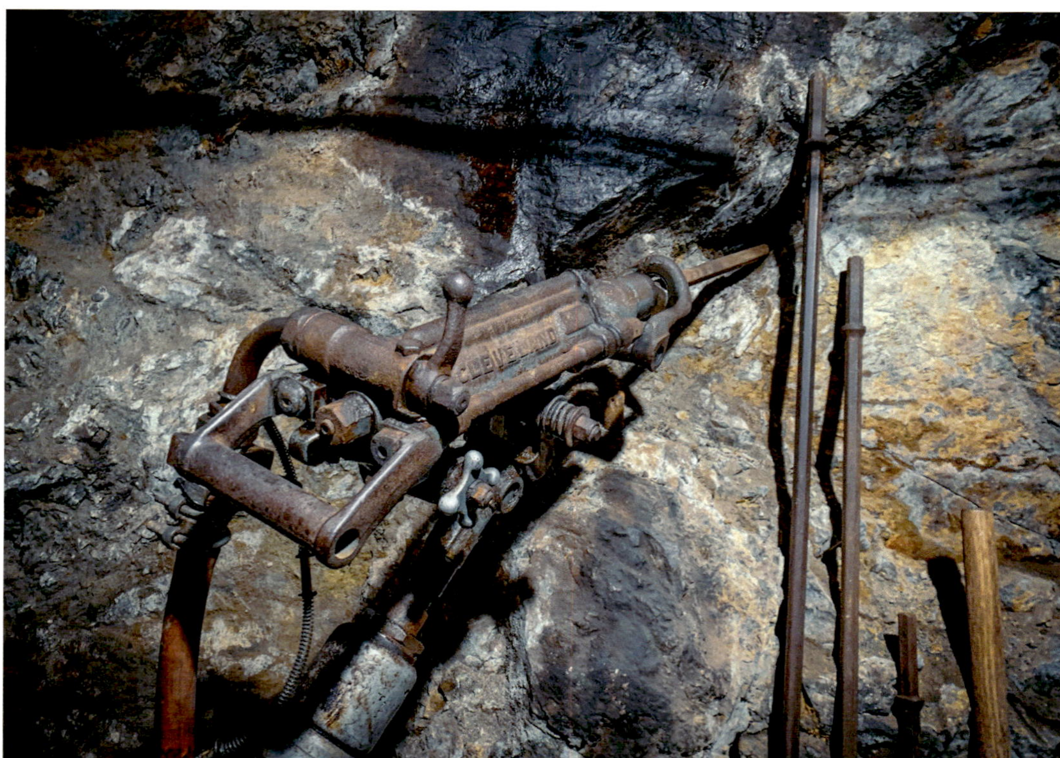

Pneumatic drills like this one replaced hand tools and dangerous, manual techniques such as "double jacking."

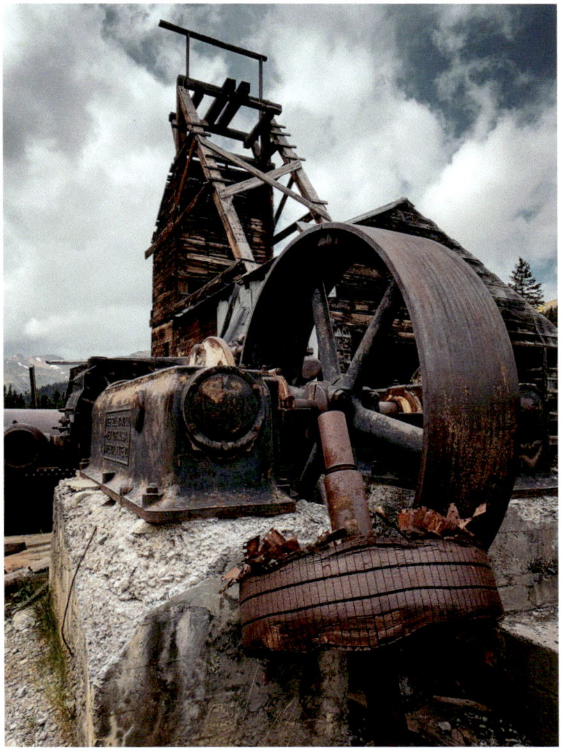

Right: A headframe and an Ingersoll-Rand compressor at the Longfellow mine, Red Mountain.

Below: Heavy, steel hoists like this one, found outside the Vindicator mine, were essential for vertical hardrock mining.

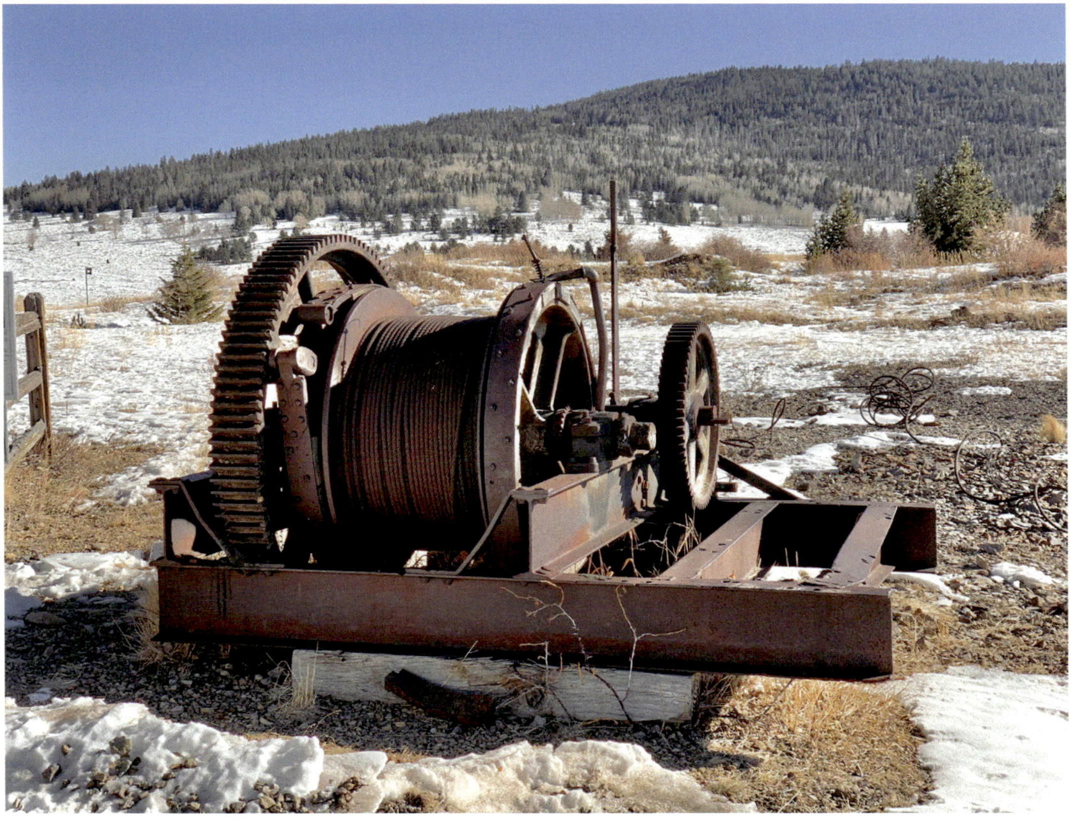

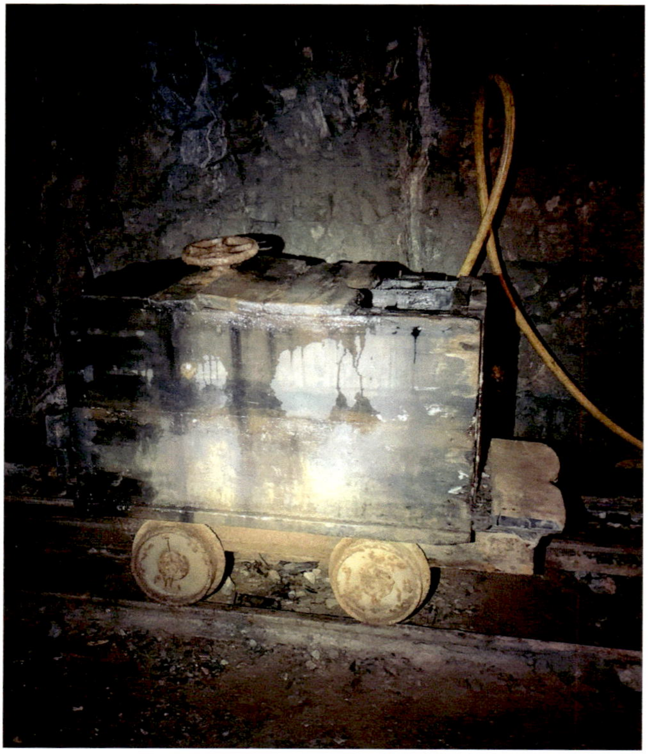

Left: Hardrock mining presented some unique challenges. When you are miles underground, it helps to have a commode on wheels.

Below: The Como roundhouse was built in 1881 to service Denver, South Park, and Pacific Railroad locomotives that made daily trips over the Boreas Pass to Breckenridge.

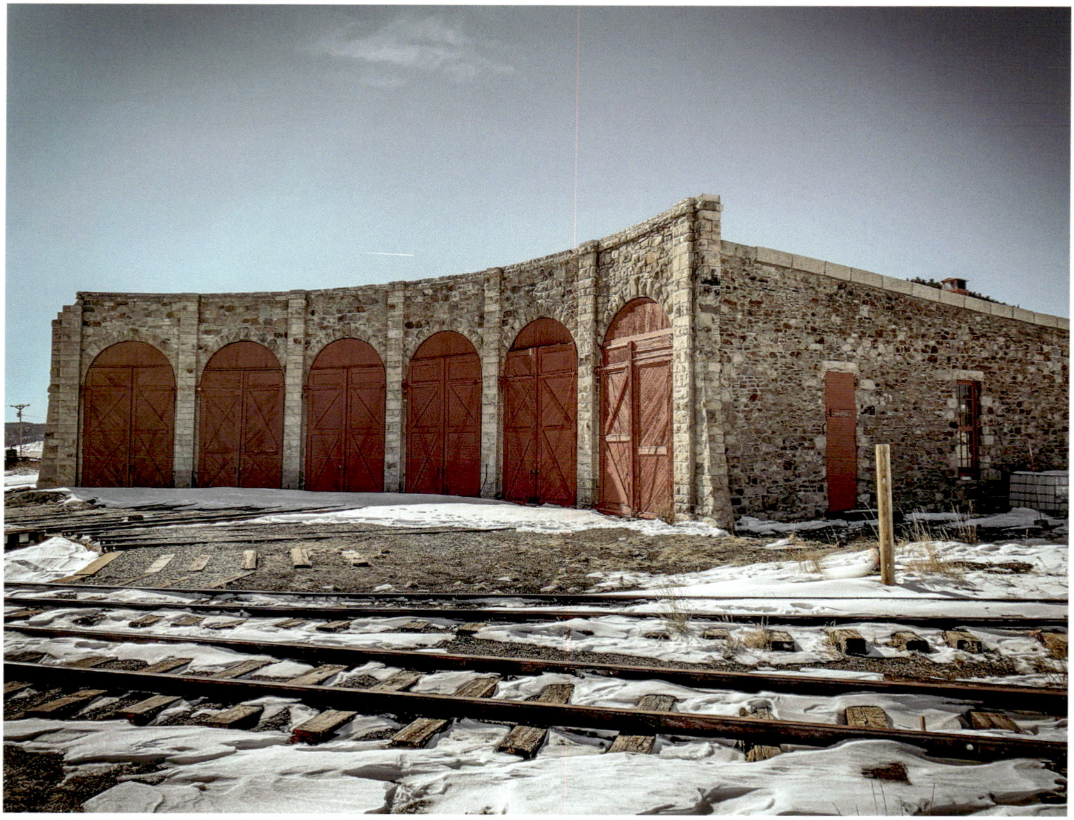

Right: A Baldwin 2-6-2 locomotive named *Klondike Kate* now resides inside the old roundhouse.

Below: The old Como rail depot is being slowly restored by one of the dying town's only residents.

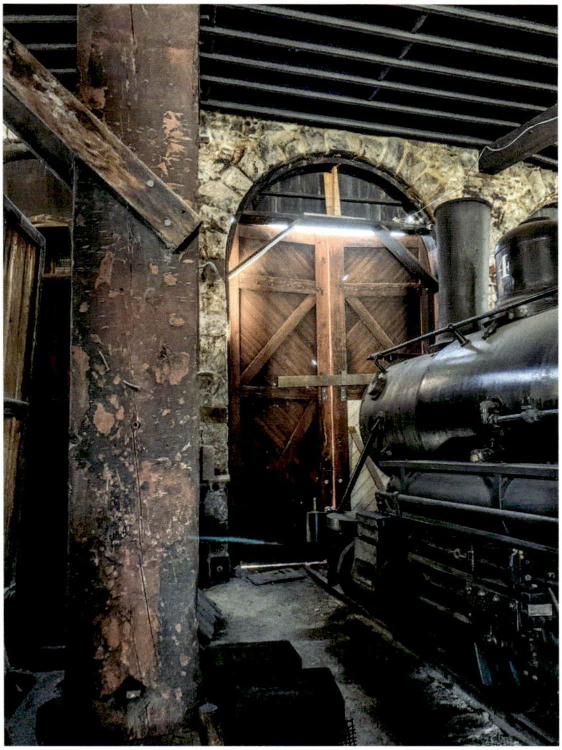

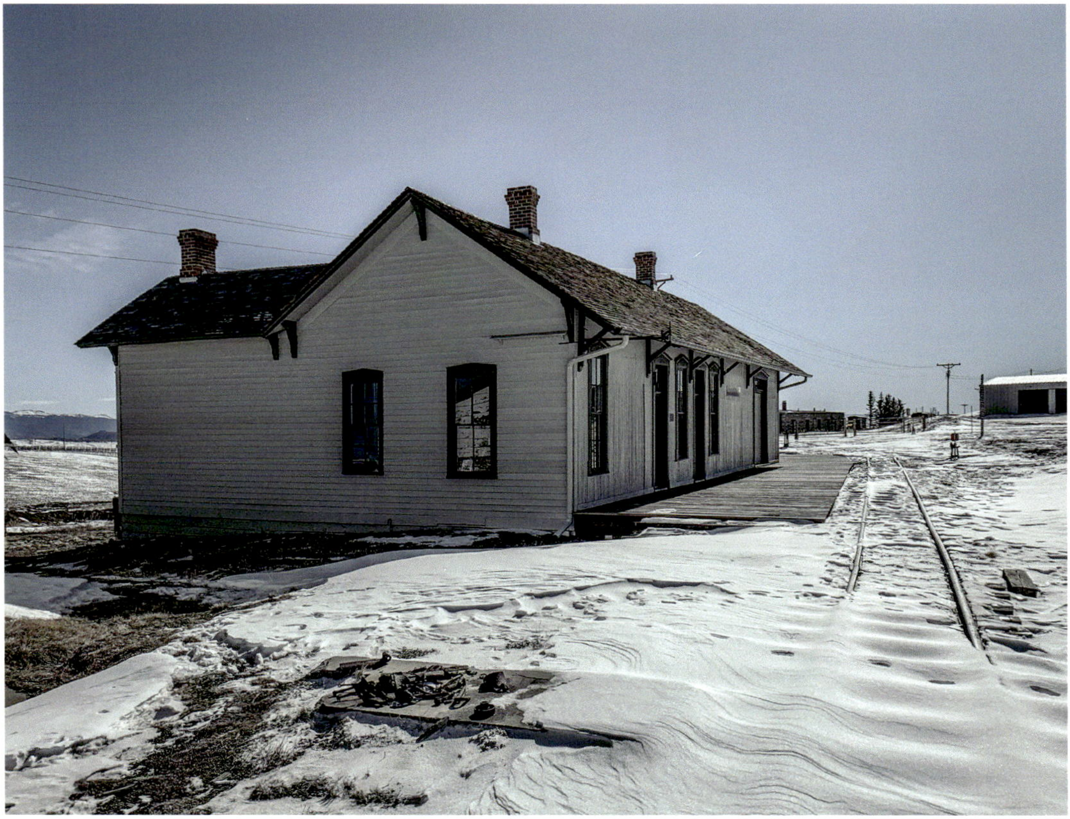

3

SILVER IS THE NEW GOLD

Overshadowed by the more highly valued gold, silver deposits had been largely ignored in Colorado. Despite often occurring in the same ore, silver was frequently discarded as waste. This changed abruptly in 1878 when Congress passed the Bland–Allison Act, authorizing the free coinage of silver. The government demand caused silver prices to skyrocket.

Just months later in 1879, major silver strikes were made in Leadville, kicking off the Colorado Silver Boom. For the second time in the young state's history, hopeful prospectors flocked to the Rockies. Many of the old, abandoned settlements were re-inhabited and new ones sprang up.

As the Leadville mines rapidly became overpopulated, two prospectors ventured west, discovering a rich vein of silver in the remote Castle Creek Valley. Others soon followed, and the respectable town of Ashcroft mushroomed in the swale. The shallow deposits played out quickly though, and the settlement was largely abandoned when promising, new strikes were made in Aspen.

Many other boom towns shared a similar story. Teller City to the north sprang up so fast that there is one account of a couple staying at the grand Yates House Hotel while it was being constructed around them. The town died just as quickly when the silver ran out. The mining settlements of Vicksburg and Winfield to the south shared similar fates.

Perhaps Colorado's most famous ghost town, St. Elmo was longer-lived than most. This was due largely to its position on the Denver, South Park, and Pacific Railroad. When the mountain pass tunnel known as the Alpine Tunnel was abandoned, however, St. Elmo became a dead-end, both literally and figuratively.

During the Pikes Peak Gold Rush, a group of brazen prospectors had ventured into the San Juan Mountains—then considered Indian territory—and discovered promising gold placers. They were quickly driven out by the Utes, but in 1873, the tribe relinquished their lands in the Brunot Agreement and the region became a hotspot for hopeful prospectors. Immediately following the Ute withdrawal, 4,000 mining claims were staked in the San Juan Mountains.

Though gold was the initial attractor, extensive silver deposits were found that coincided conveniently well with the impending boom. Several settlements sprang up along the Animas River in support of the new mines. This included one of Colorado's best-preserved ghost towns—Animas Forks.

Though not in the immediate vicinity of any substantial mineral prospects, Animas Forks survived largely on speculative investment. Just on the other side of Houghton Mountain, a rich, 60-foot-thick quartz vein had been discovered at an isolated mining camp known as Mineral Point. The Dakota and San Juan Mining Company intended to build a mill there, but the mountainous terrain made moving materials all but impossible. Animas Forks, being far more accessible, was chosen instead, cementing the humble camp's place on the map. Unfortunately, by the time the mill was completed, mining at Mineral Point had become unfeasibly expensive. The new facility never operated consistently enough to be profitable, but its very presence gave the town of Animas Forks an air of success.

In 1877, an investor named Franklin Josiah Pratt intended to reach the elusive ore bodies beneath Mineral Point via a 3-mile-long tunnel dug from Animas Forks. As workers and their families flooded in, the humble alpine camp blossomed into a respectable town. For many years, it served as a central hub for the Eureka Mining District.

By 1884, Pratt's Bonanza Tunnel, as it came to be known, had still not produced an ounce of ore. The decision was made to abandon the project and the town quickly followed suit after a fire destroyed the business district in 1891. Animas Forks would later see a major revival when gold was discovered to be in the same ore that had been previously mined for silver. The town played host to two more major milling operations: The Gold Prince Mill, the most expensive mill built in Colorado to that time, and a prefabricated, 150-ton concentration facility known as the Frisco Mill. While the Gold Prince was torn down to build the Eureka mine downriver, the Frisco Mill still stands to this day.

Despite countless, substantial mineral strikes, the San Juan mines were significantly handicapped by their seclusion. Many claims sat well above 10,000 feet, and miners were forced to abandon their operations during the long and harsh winters. When ore could be extracted, it had to be transported great distances by mule, over steep and narrow passes. Most operations were just not economically feasible without the support of civilization.

The Denver and Rio Grande Railway reached Silverton in 1882, ending the frustrating waiting game. District production went from $15,000 in 1874 to $400,000 in 1883. By 1885, it had reached $1 million per year and continued to climb. Spur lines reached Telluride and Red Mountain around 1890, connecting these highly lucrative regions with the rest of the world.

The arrival of the railroad in the San Juan Mountains made viable some of the most profitable mining operations in the state. In the slapdash town of Guston, the Yankee Girl mine was so successful that the owners were able to pay nearly $1 million in dividends. Other mines in the Red Mountain District—such as the Genessee, Guston-Robinson, Vanderbilt, and National Belle—saw similar success, coaxing several new settlements into existence.

High above Telluride, the Smuggler-Union mine was flourishing. Like many of the more remote, alpine operations, the mine did not benefit from direct proximity to the railroad but instead used an elaborate tram system to transport ore down to civilization. The neighboring town of Tomboy built a massive mill to process ore on-site. While most of the higher elevation settlements were vacated during the harsh winters, Tomboy grew large enough to retain its population year-round. The town sported a Y.M.C.A. and a dancehall, offering free admission to female patrons.

In 1890, Congress passed the Sherman Silver Purchase Act. Like the Bland–Allison Act of 1878, the statute required the U.S. government to buy millions of ounces of silver in an effort to curb deflation. Although the measure gave a boost to the Colorado silver mines, it quickly developed unintended consequences. Investors began redeeming silver notes for gold, and within a few years, federal gold reserves were at their minimum statutory limits.

Attempting to alleviate the economic strain, President Grover Cleveland repealed the Sherman Purchase Act in 1893. The decision proved disastrous. Overnight, silver prices plummeted, creating a catastrophic ripple effect throughout the economy. Some 15,000 businesses, 500 banks, and nearly all the major railroads went bankrupt. The stock market crashed and unemployment surged to 19 percent.

No state was affected more by the Panic of 1893 than Colorado. As the silver mines shut down, entire towns were left fallow. The state economy effectively came to a standstill and thousands were left unemployed. Even famed mining tycoon Horace Tabor lost his entire fortune, dying penniless a few years later. The Colorado Silver Boom was over and the state was in turmoil.

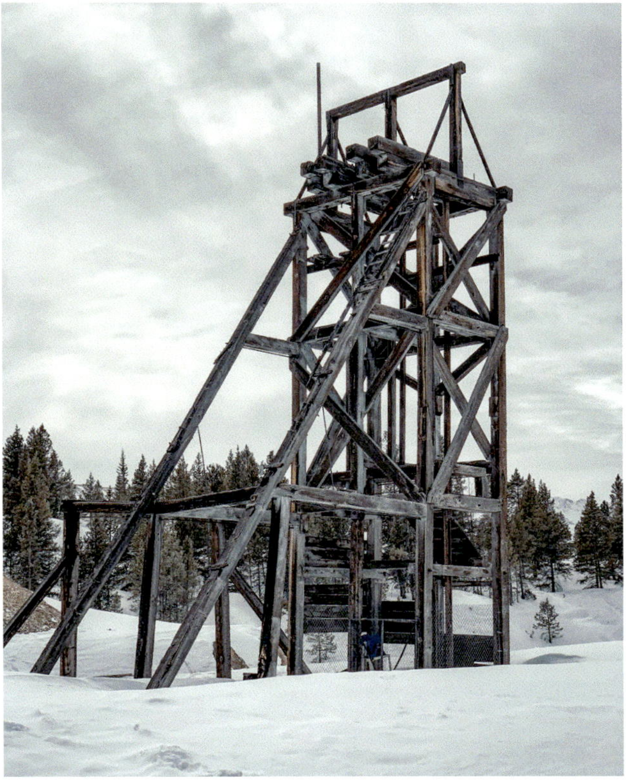

The Robert Emmet mine headframe in Leadville.

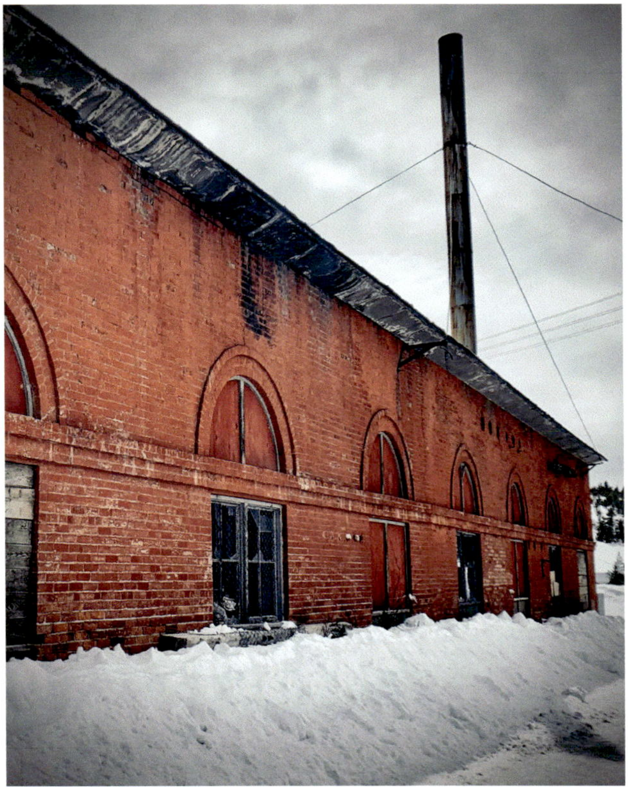

The Yak Power Plant in Leadville was one of the earliest in the country, using steam to provide electricity to the nearby mines.

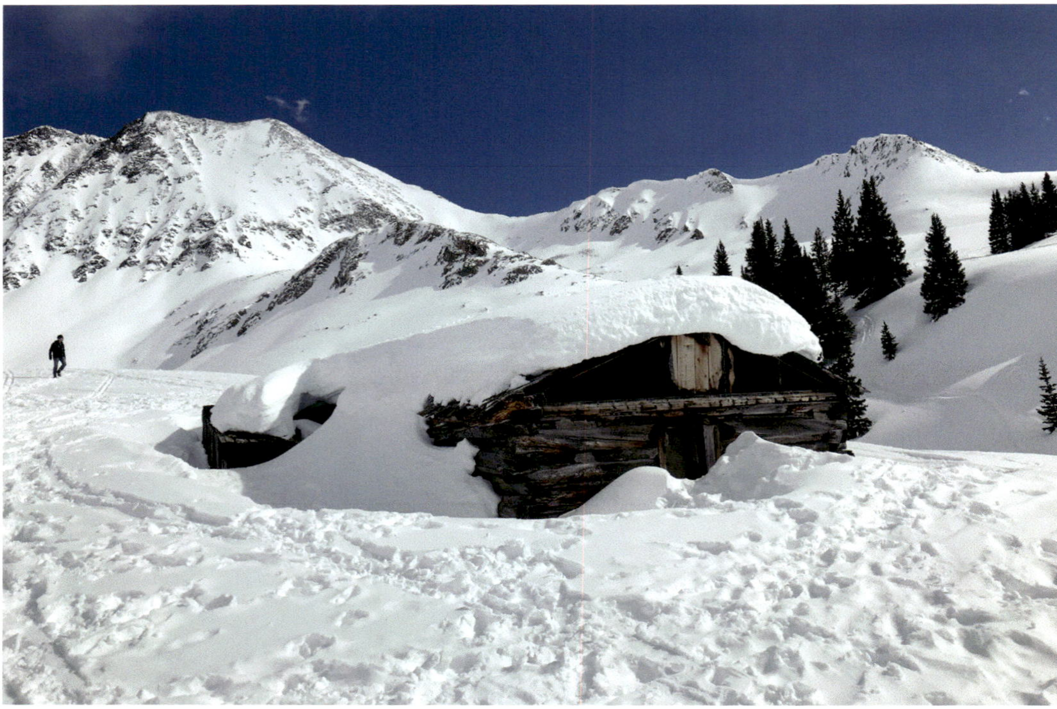

Snow envelops a log structure at the Boston mining camp. A mineral vein containing gold, silver, and lead was discovered here in 1884, shortly after the Silver Boom began.

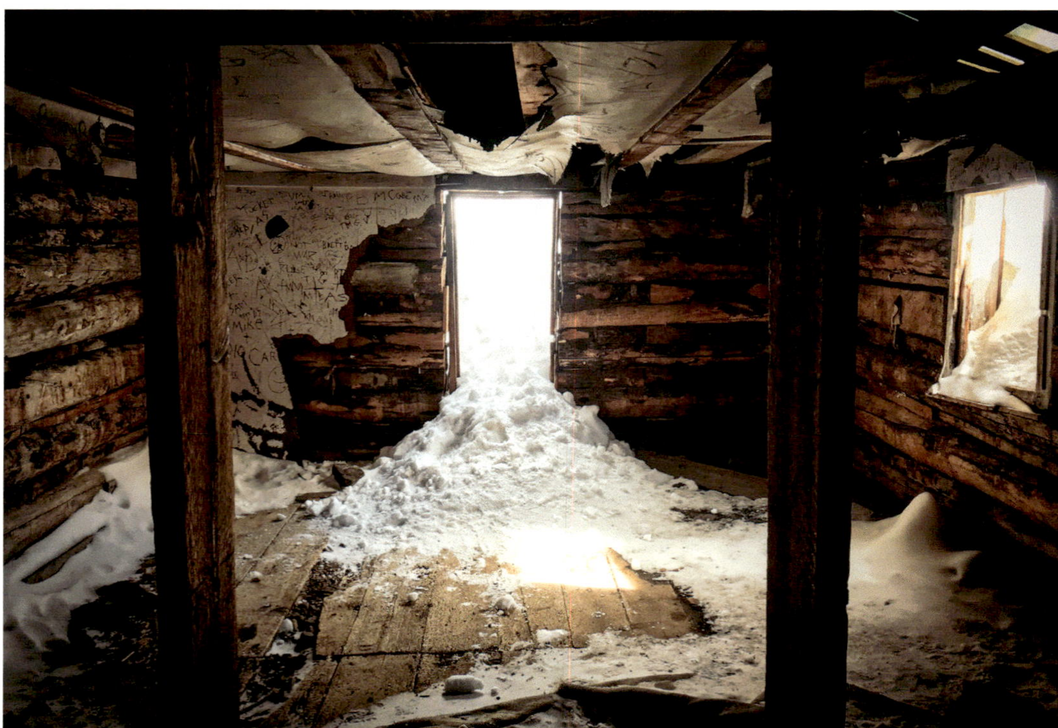

Harsh winters and low-grade ore led to the eventual abandonment of the Boston mining operation.

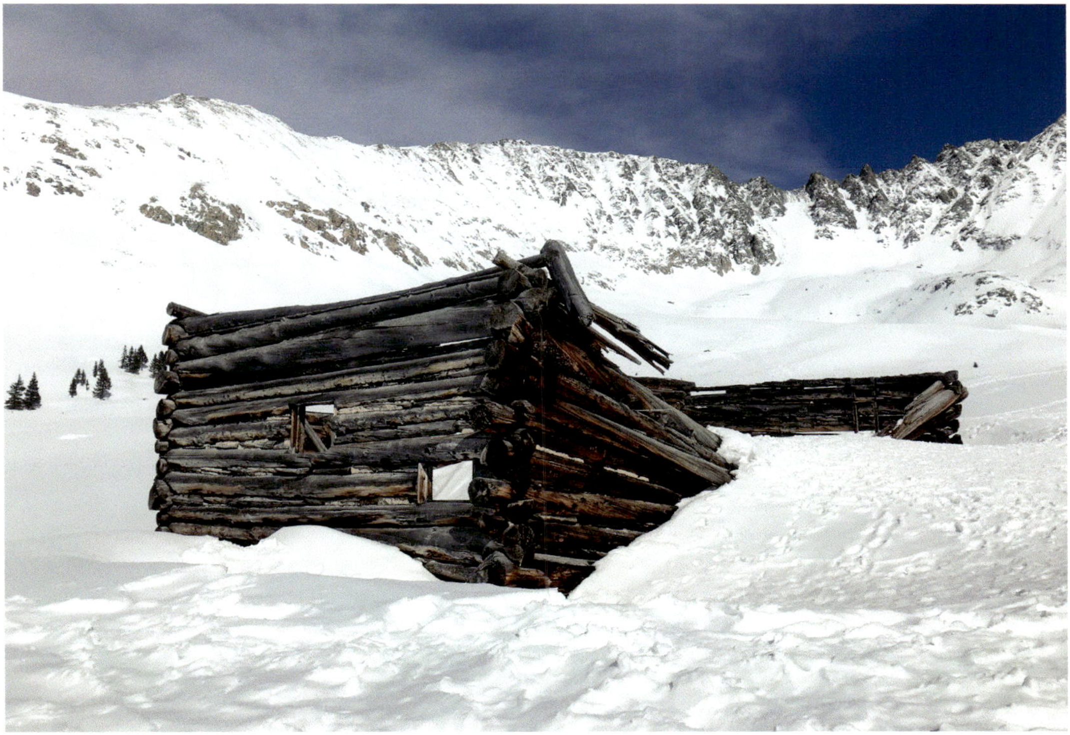

A collapsed bunkhouse in Mayflower Gulch.

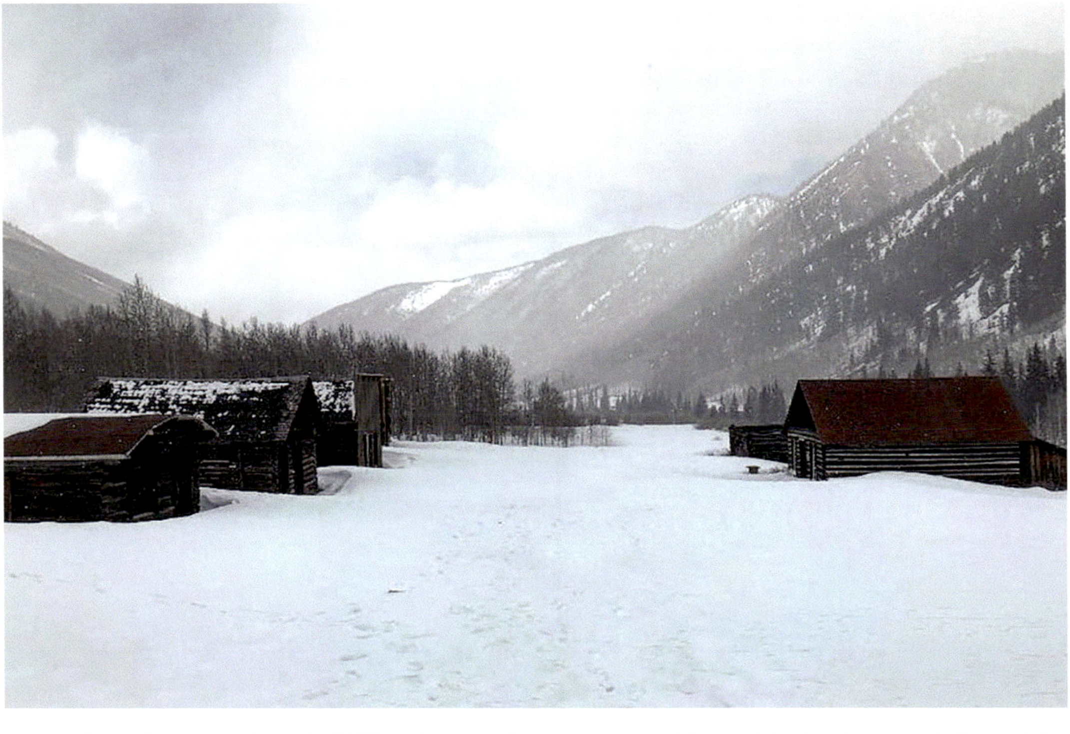

Ashcroft was once home to 3,500 residents and became successful enough to draw investments from mining tycoon H. A. W. Tabor, who hosted a grand ball in town.

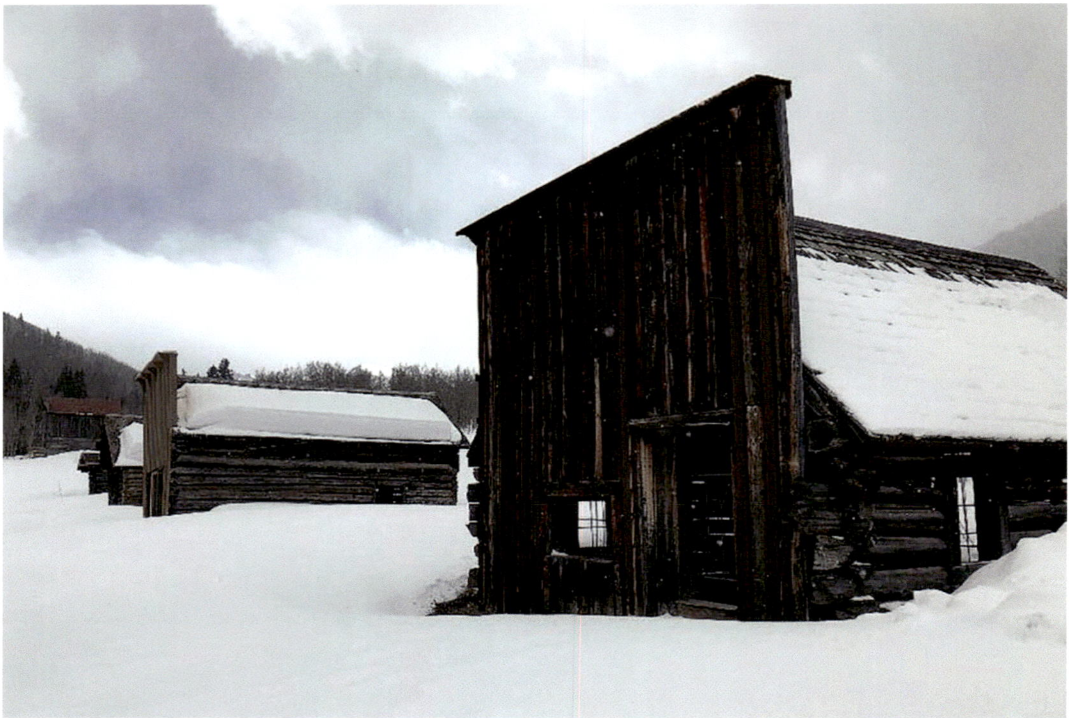

In 1955, long after being abandoned, the remaining structures in Ashcroft were used as a filming location for the television series *Sergeant Preston of the Yukon.*

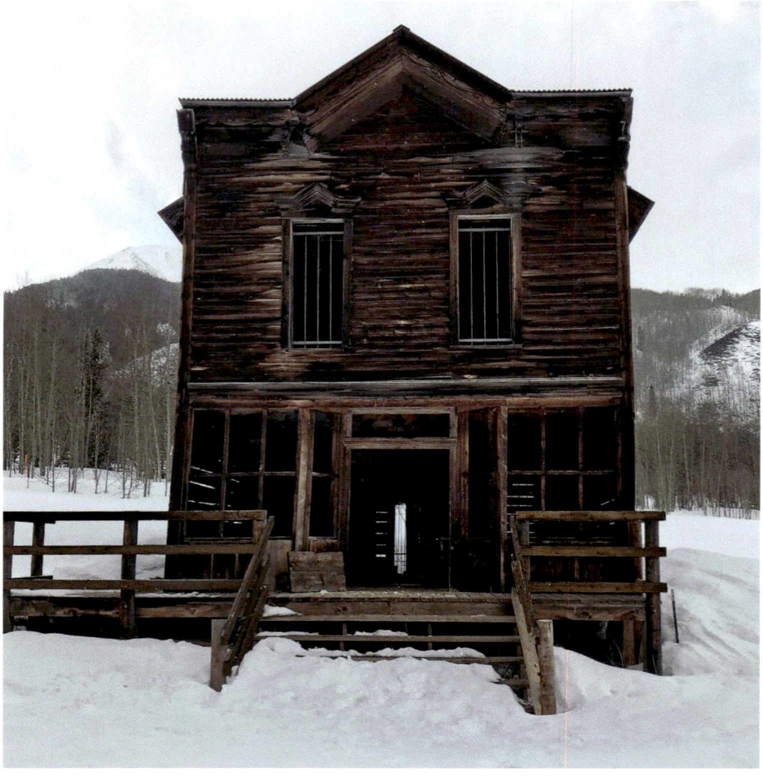

The "Hotel View" was one of more than a dozen hotels that once lined the streets of Ashcroft.

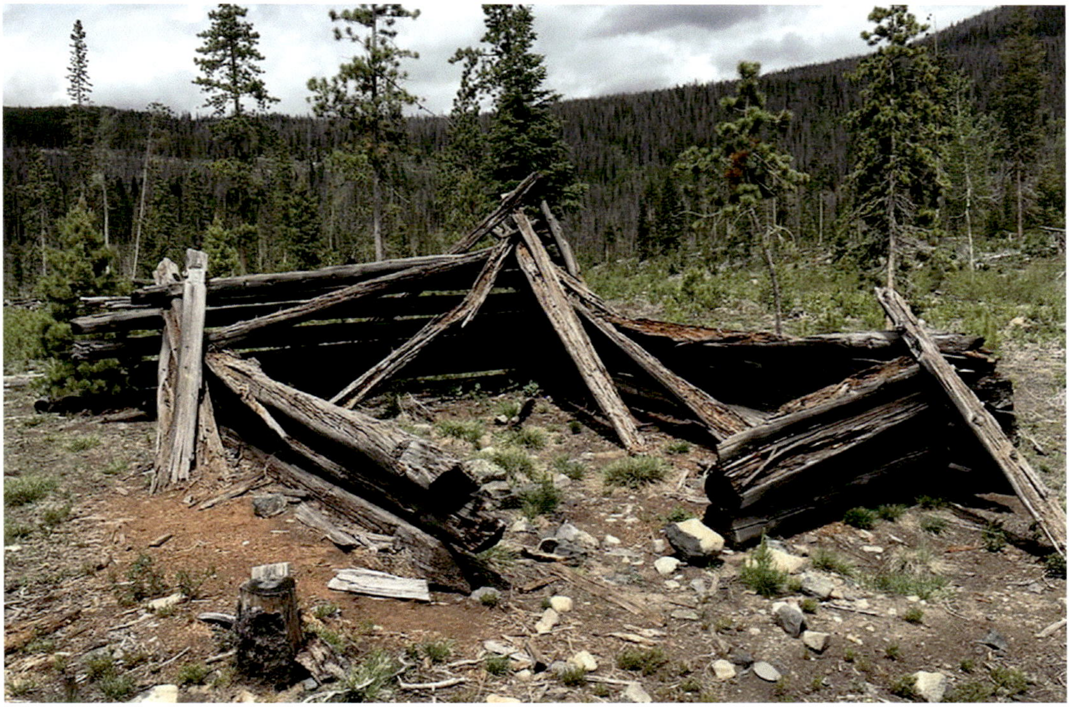

Like many alpine boom towns, Teller City was comprised largely of slapdash, stacked log structures.

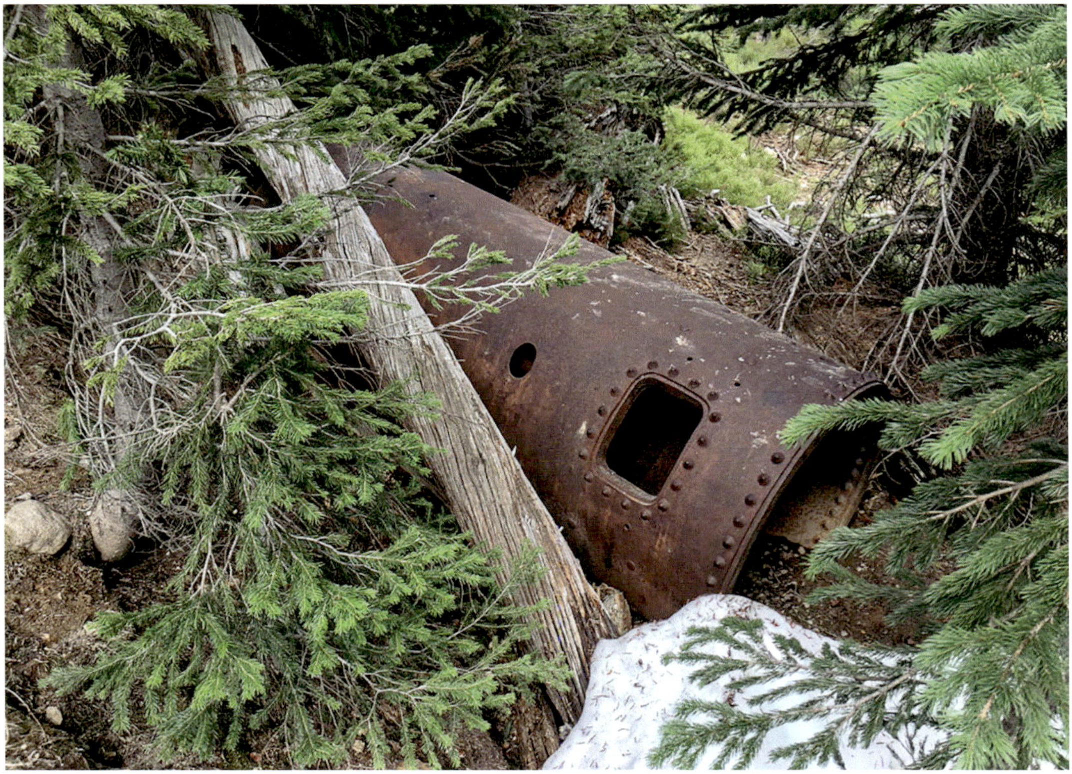

Old mining equipment like this boiler is scattered in the hills around Teller City.

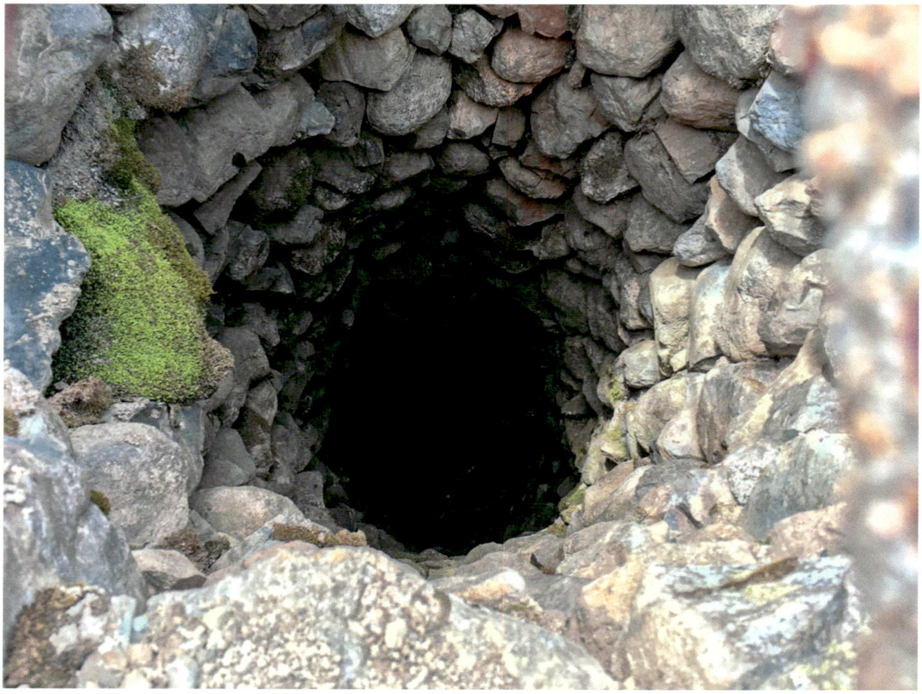

The Teller City well.

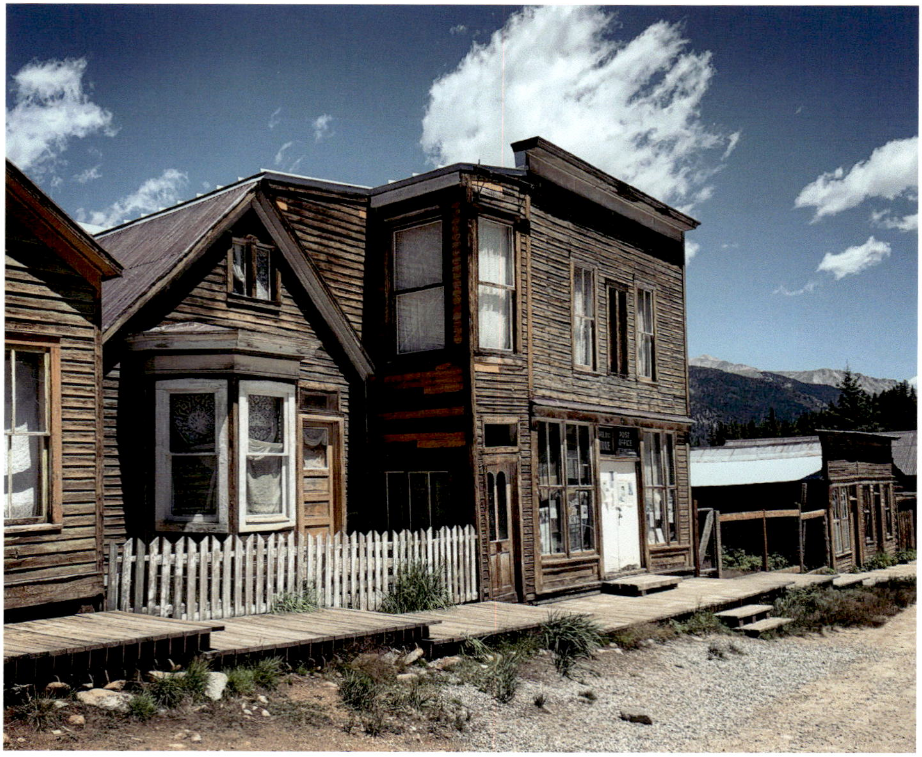

Pictured center is the home and store of the Stark family, the last residents of St. Elmo. It is said to be the most haunted structure in town.

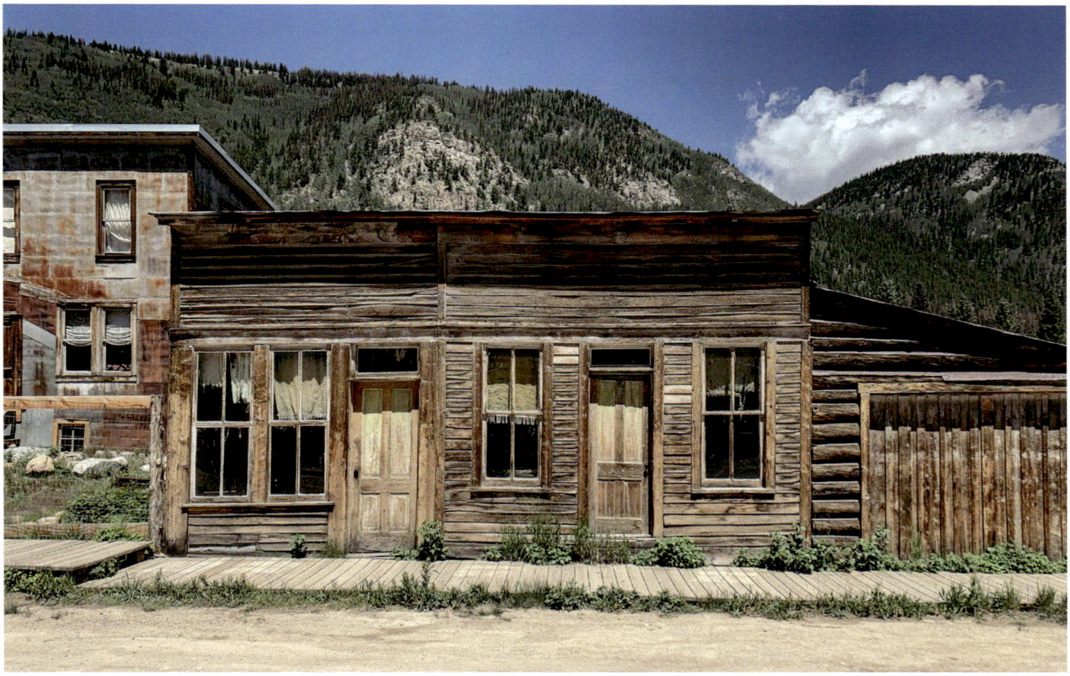

With its main street of flat-front buildings still largely intact, St. Elmo is undoubtedly one of Colorado's best-preserved ghost towns.

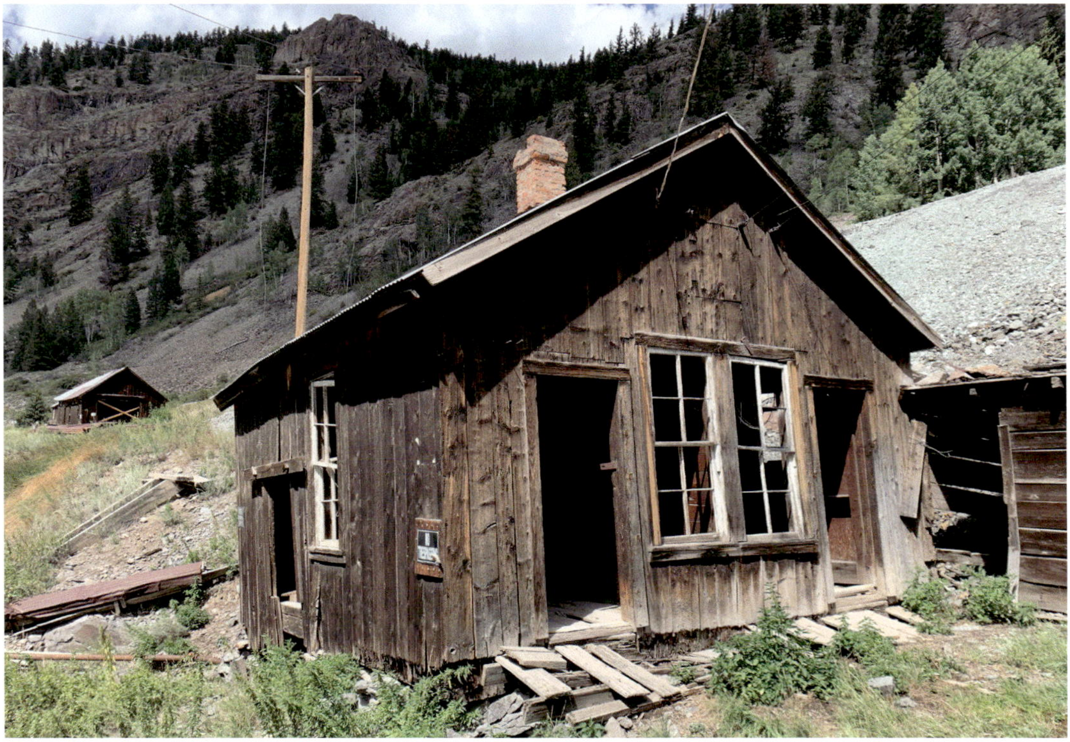

The mining town of Henson, named after one of several prospectors who trespassed into Ute territory in search of gold, but instead found silver and lead.

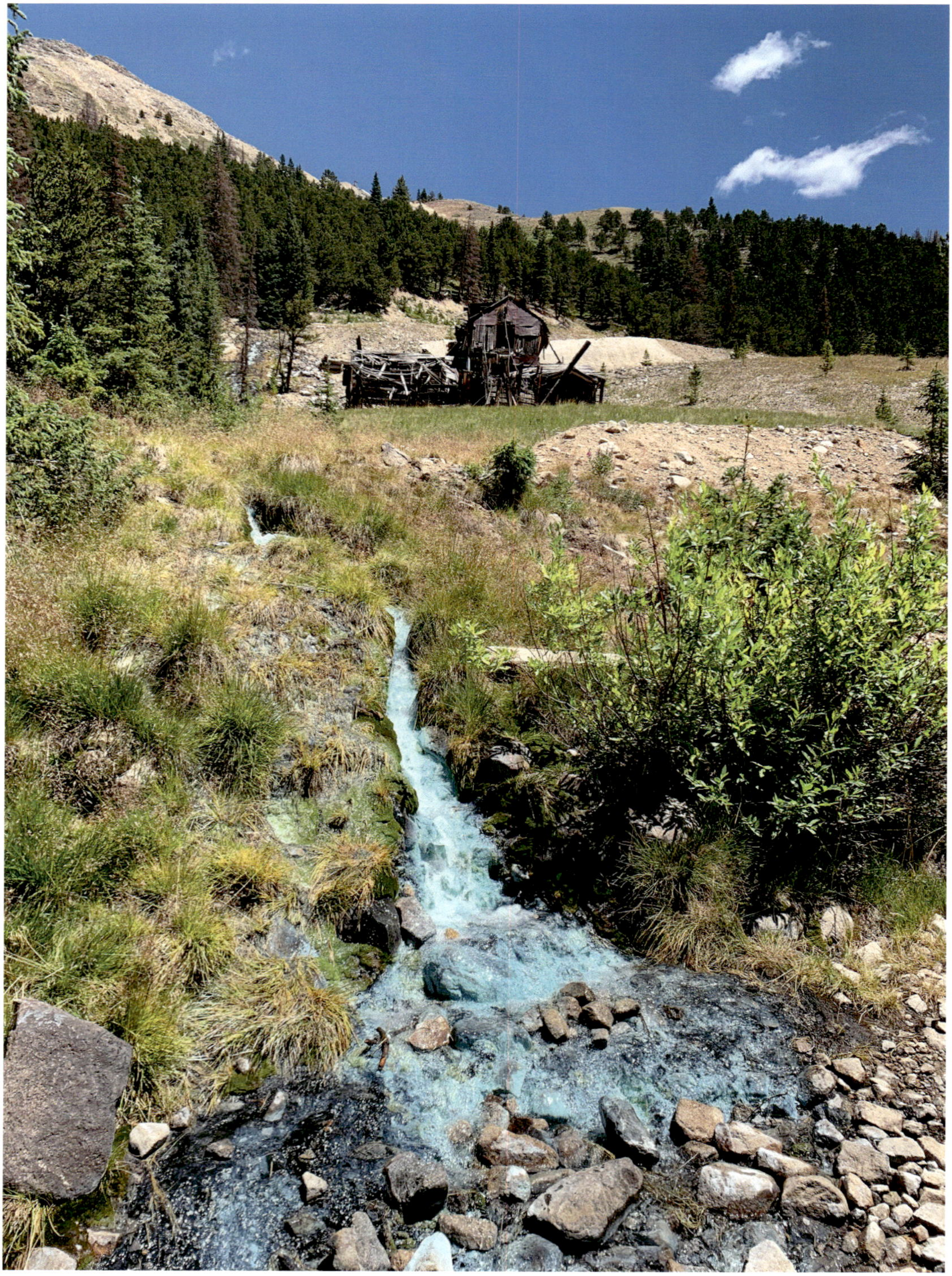

The Mary Murphy mine was by far the largest producer in the Chalk Creek Mining District, producing nearly 7 tons of pure gold by the time of its closure in 1925.

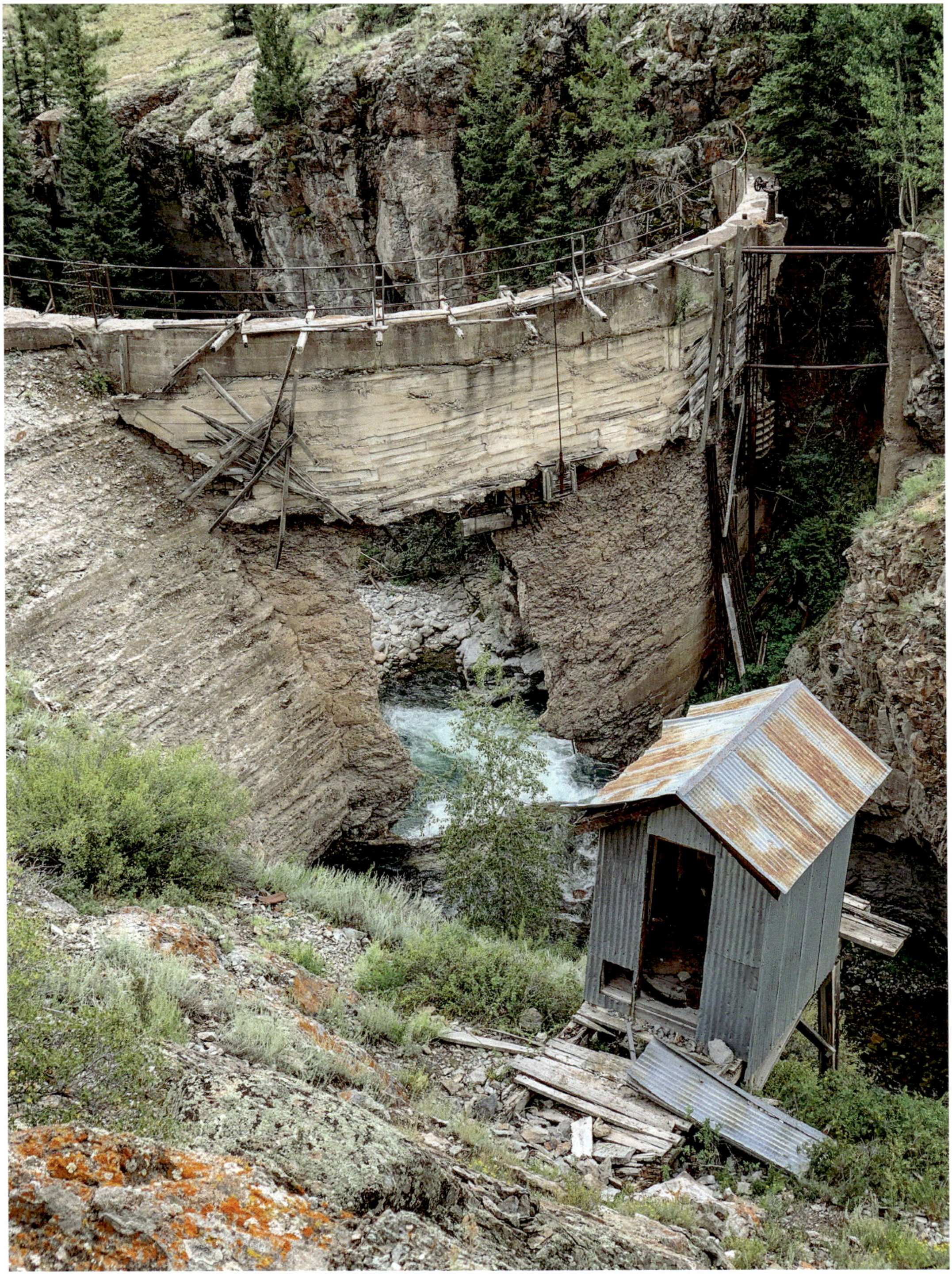

This since-breached dam once provided water for the Ute-Ulay Mill.

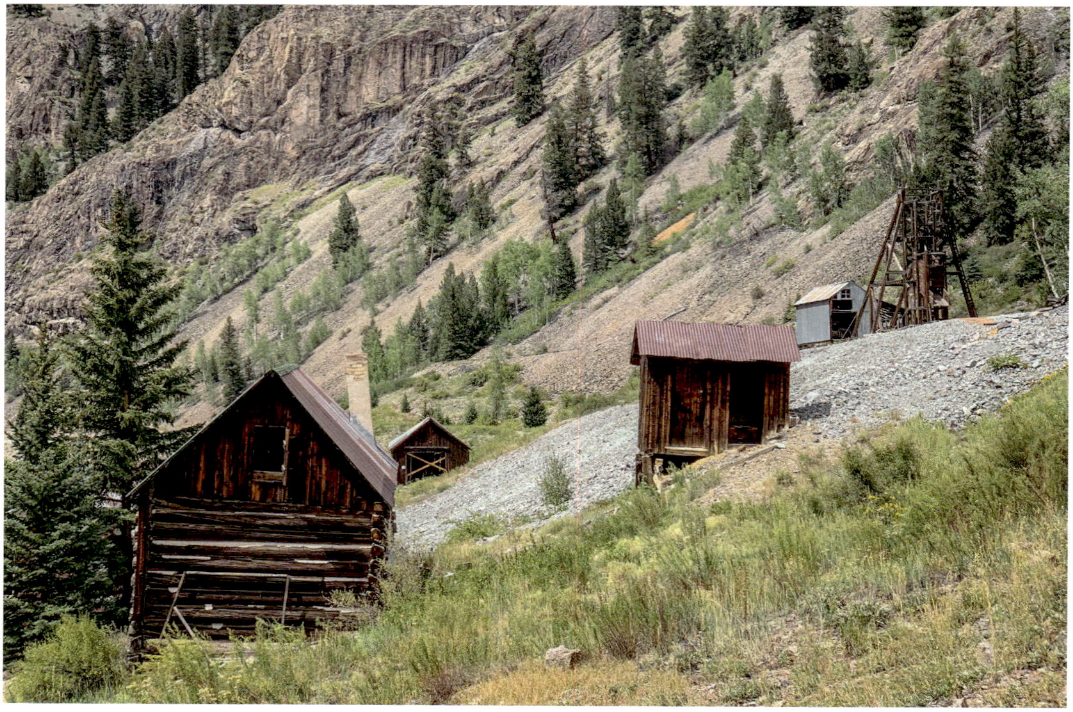

The Ute-Ulay mine, so named for the land's previous inhabitants.

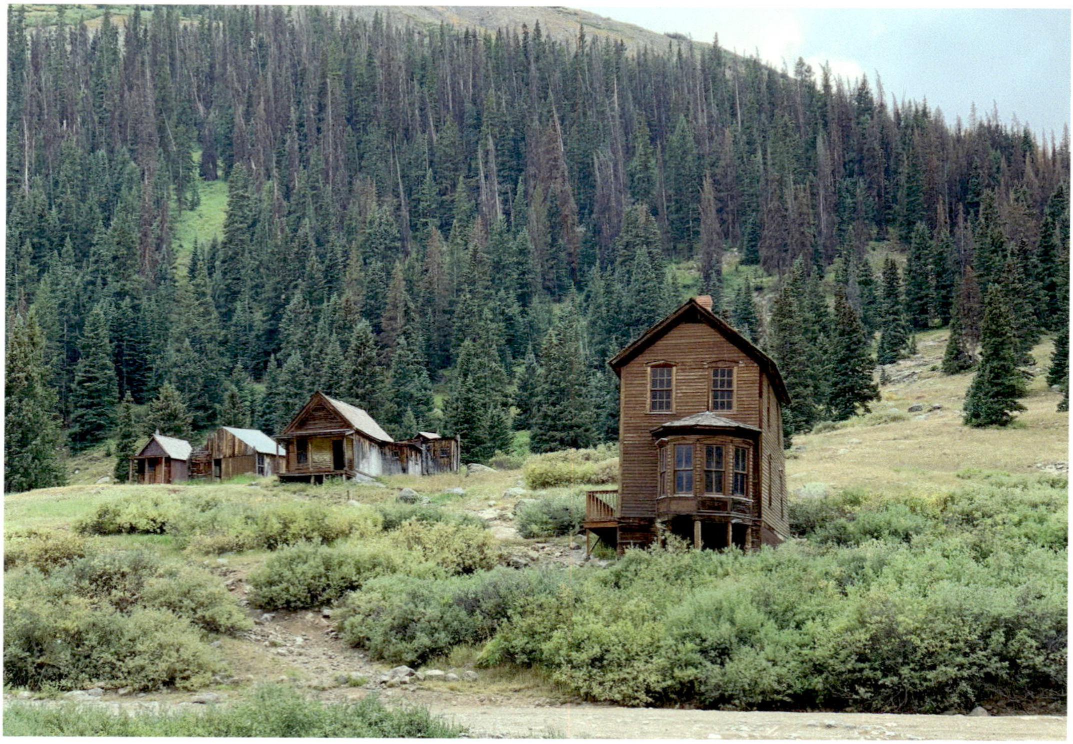

The home of William Duncan (foreground), built in 1879. Two stories high and featuring a bay window, it is certainly the grandest of the remaining structures in Animas Forks.

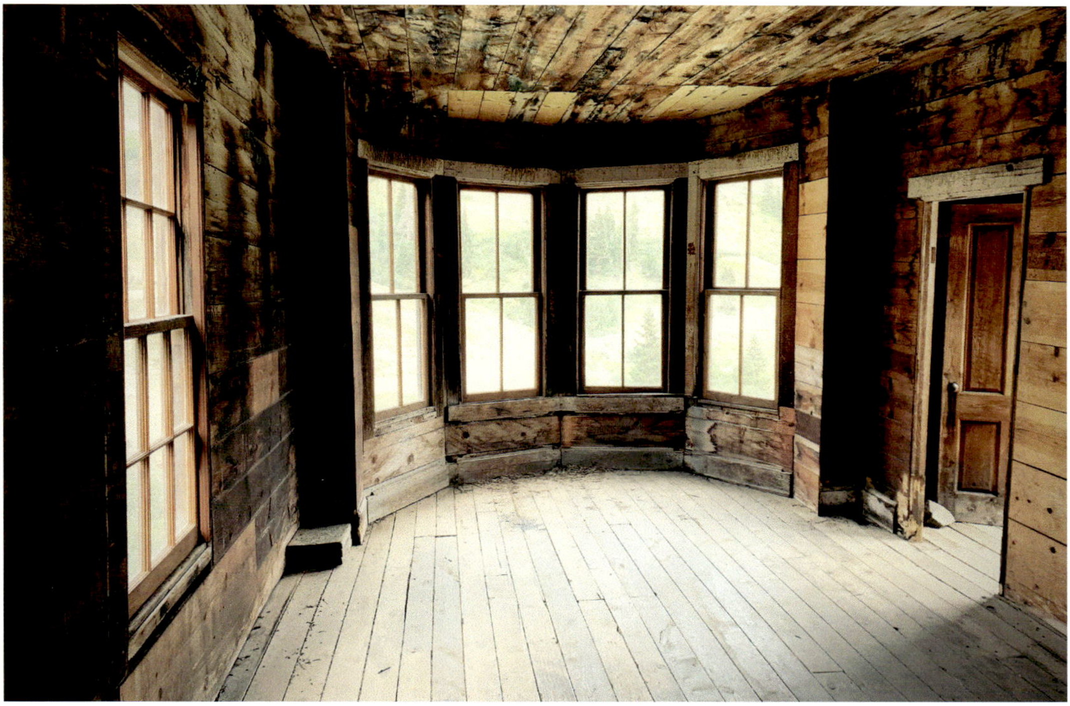

The parlor of the Duncan house.

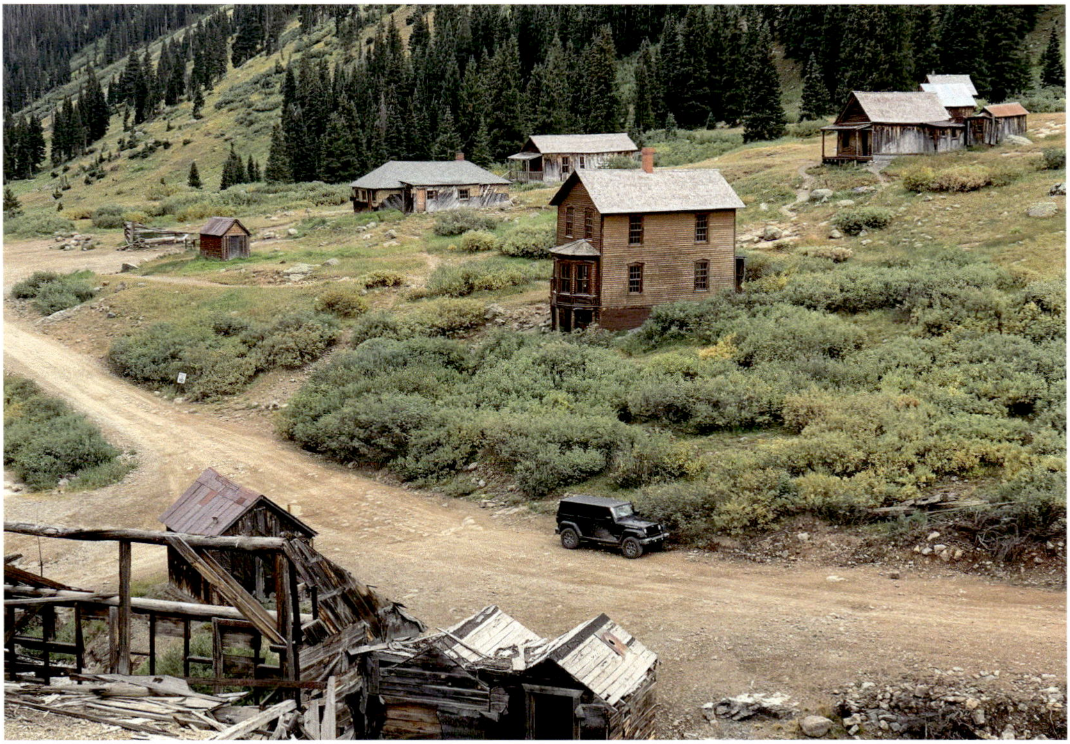

Animas Forks was ravaged by two fires, destroying much of the business district. Still, many structures have survived to the present.

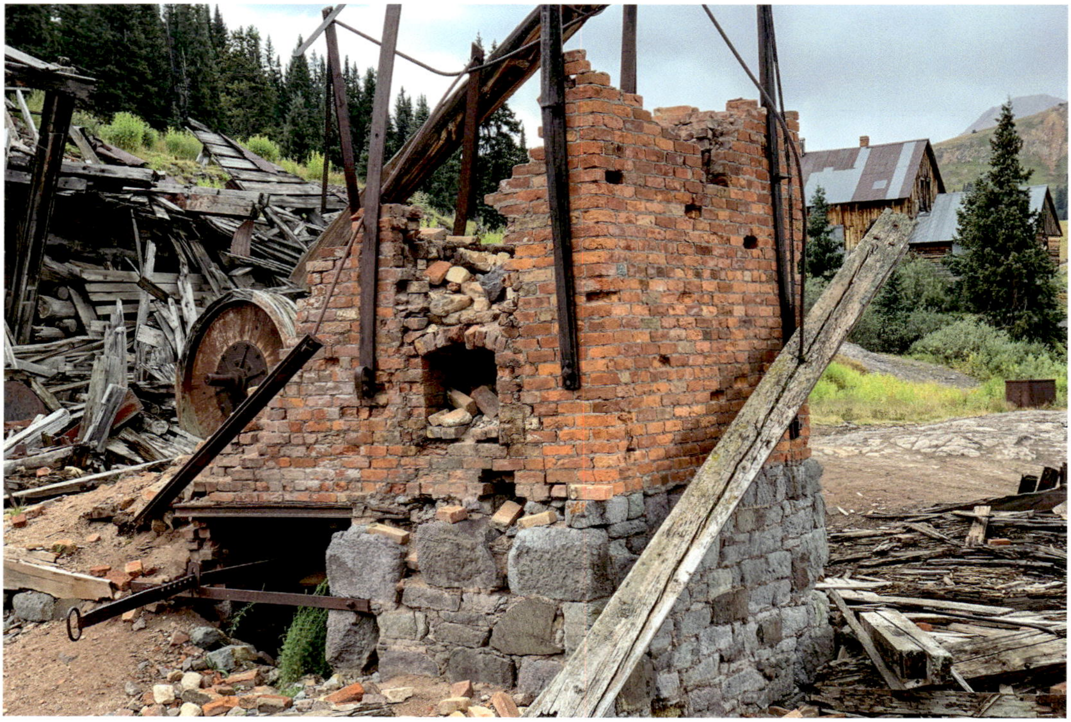

A collapsed mill at Mineral Point.

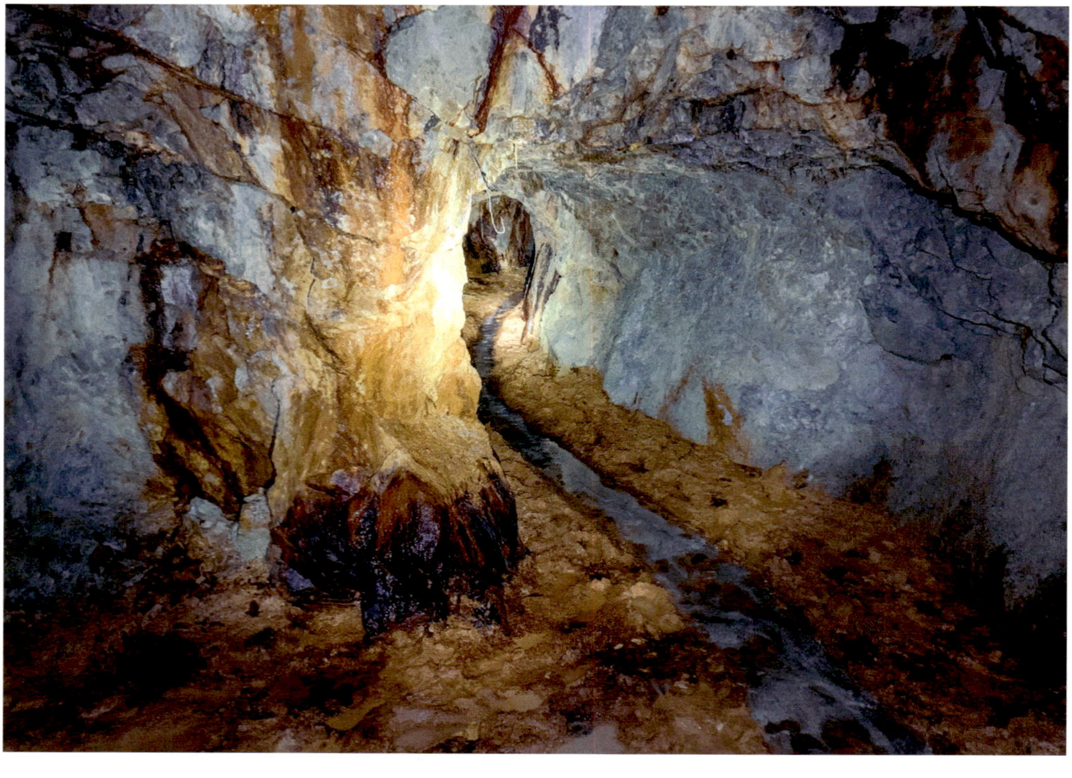

Deep inside a particularly wet mine at Mineral Point.

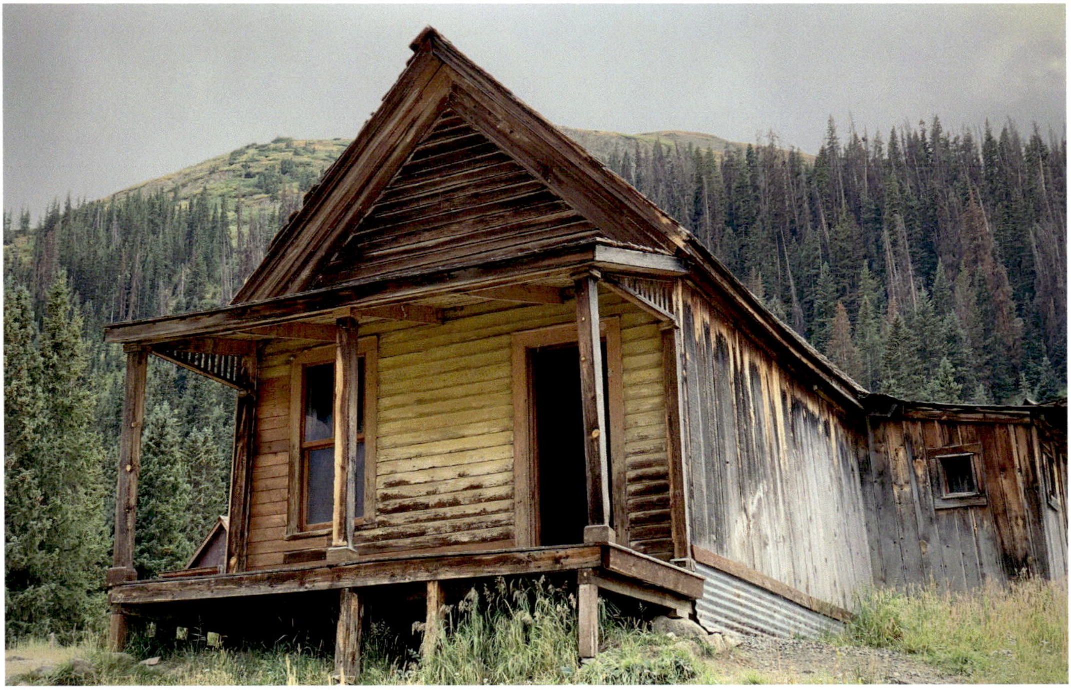

The family that lived here was one of the few that chose to remain in town during the harsh winters. The snowfall was so heavy that tunnels had to be dug between structures to get around.

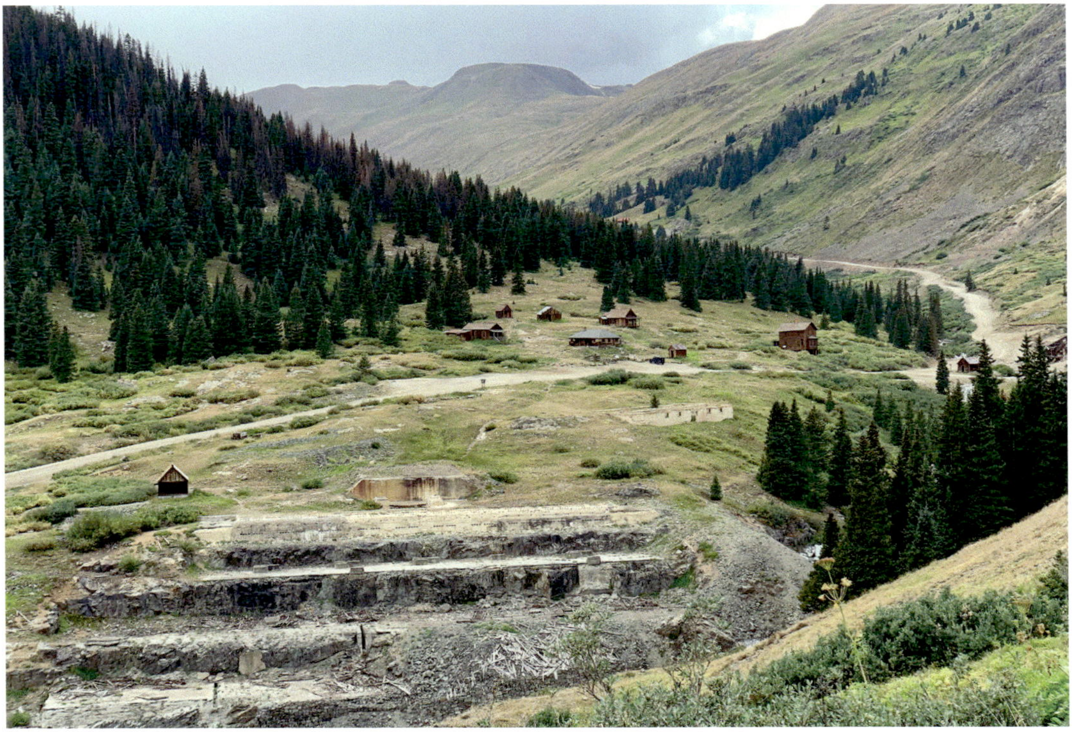

A massive, concrete foundation is all that remains of the Gold Prince Mill. The state-of-the-art structure cost $500,000 to construct and was built from steel rather than timber.

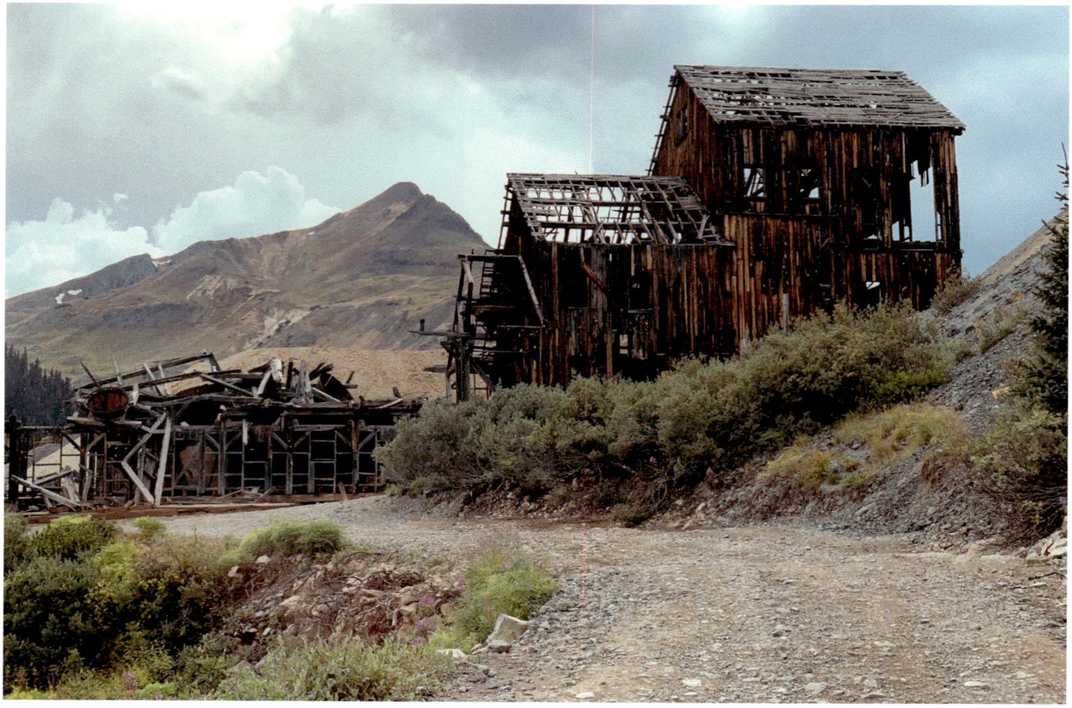

The Frisco Mill was a 150-ton, concentration mill, built in 1912 to process ore from the Bagley (Bonanza) Tunnel.

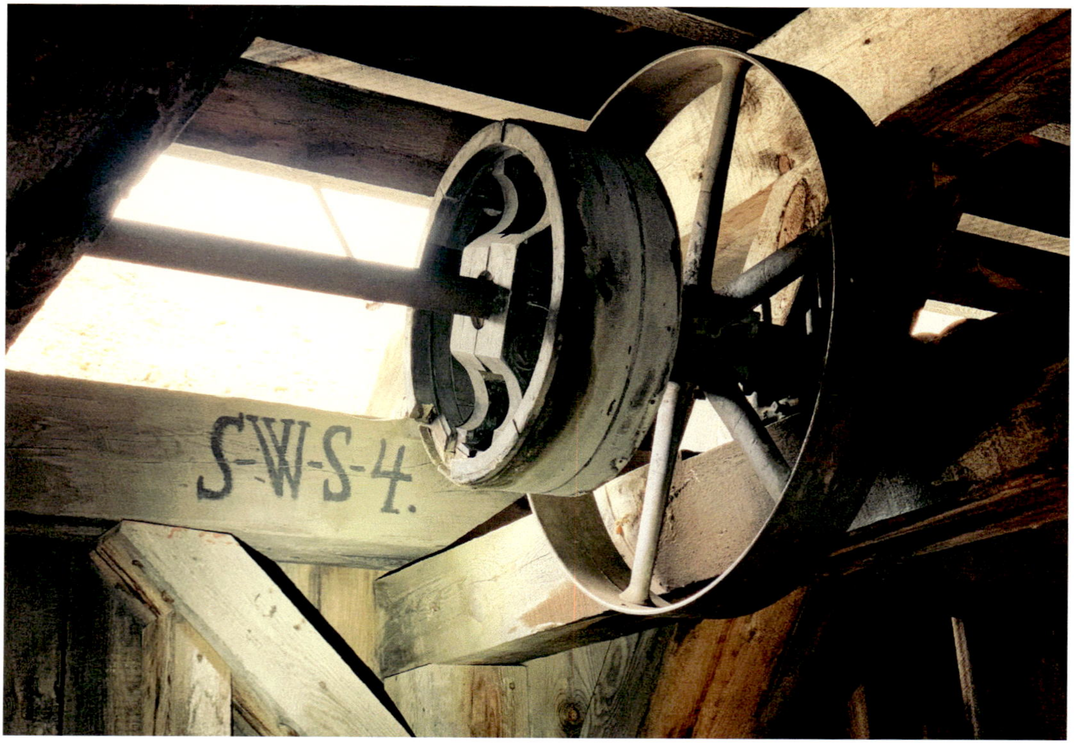

The Frisco Mill was a prefabricated building, one of the first of its kind. Painted assembly codes can be found all over the structure.

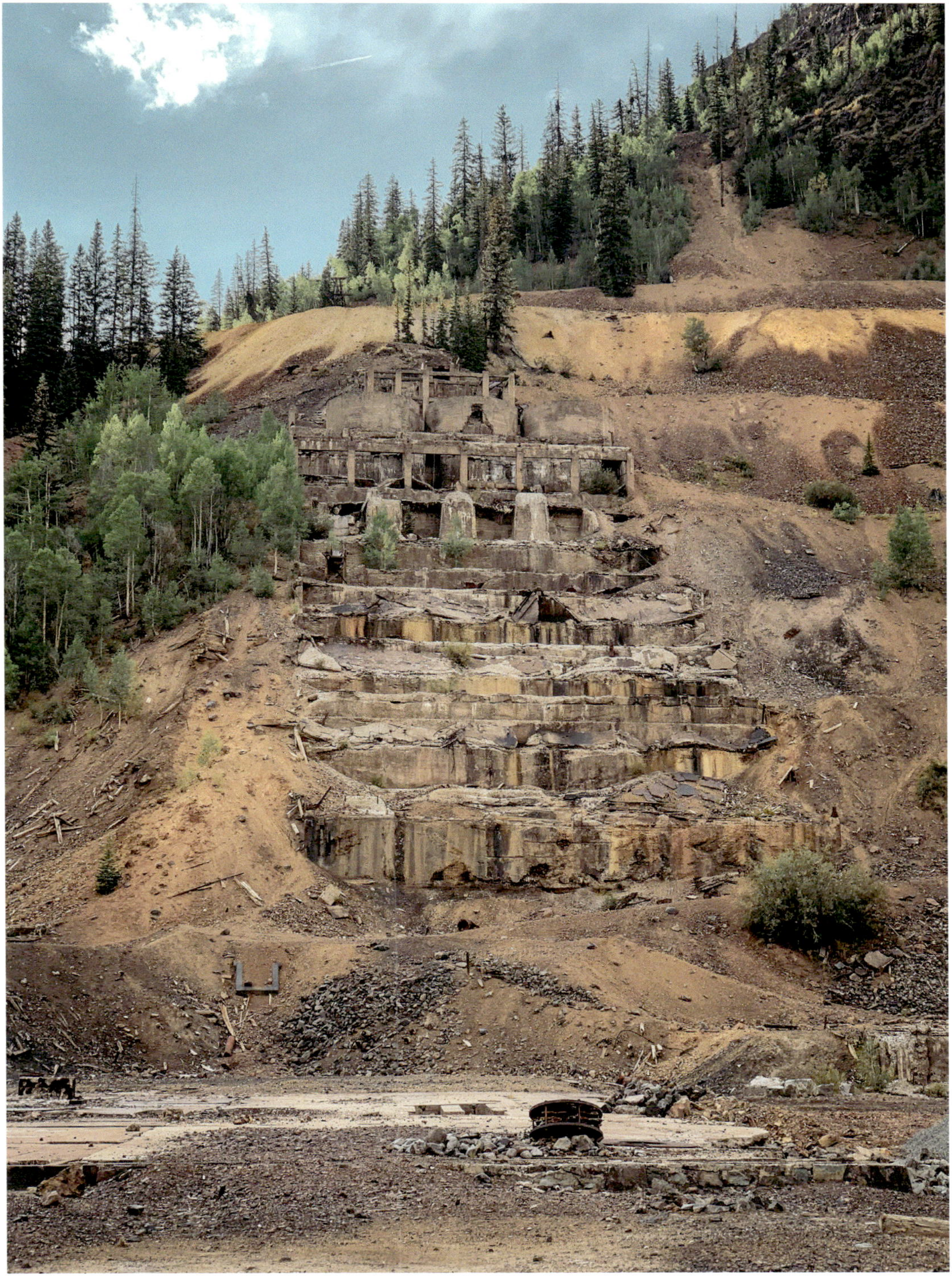

The foundation of the Eureka Mill, built in 1917 out of steel salvaged from the Gold Prince Mill.

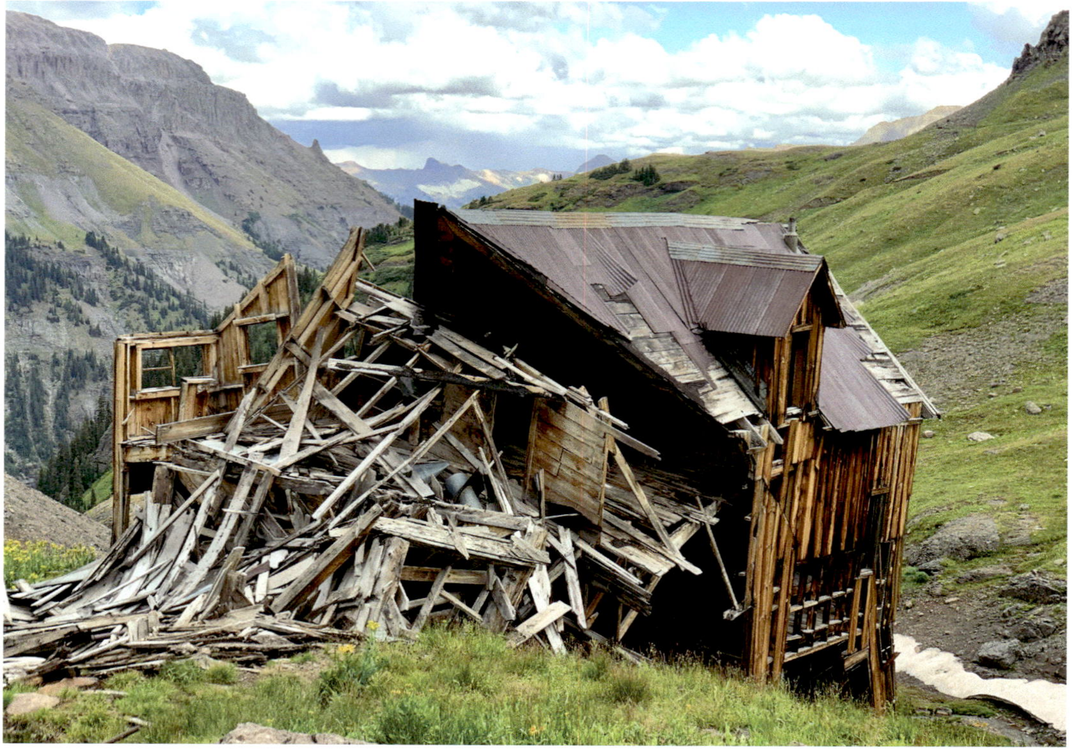

One bad winter will surely raze the old Mountain Top mine boardinghouse.

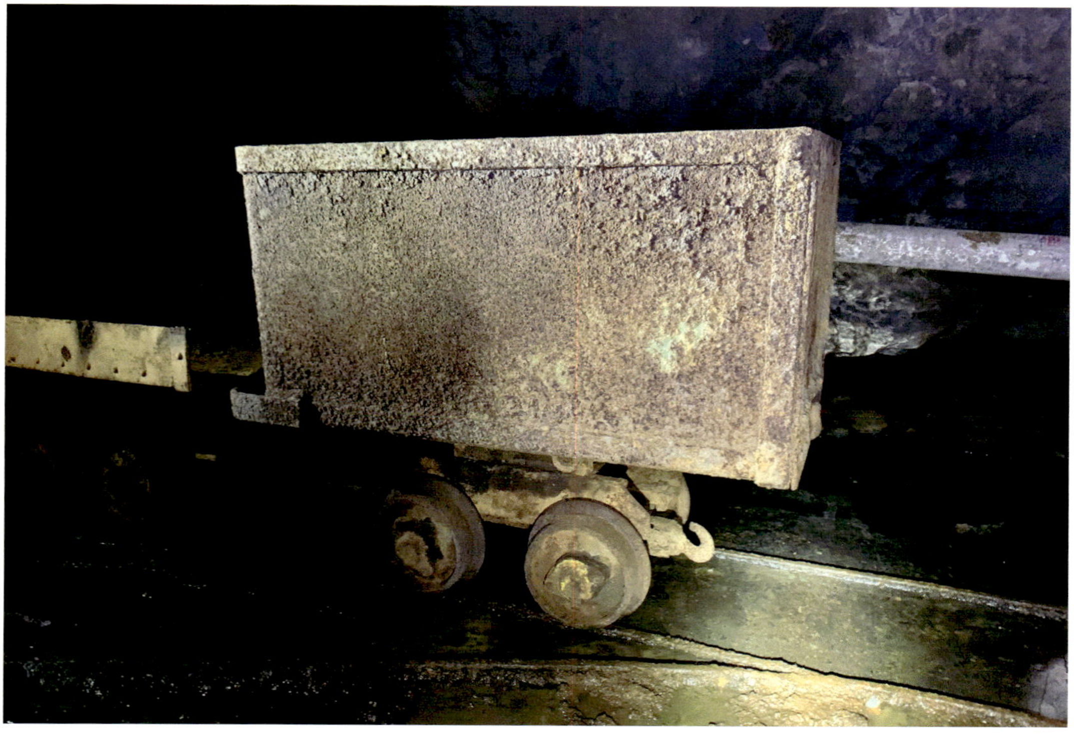

An ore cart sits inside the Mountain Top mine, one of the first and only operations to utilize an underground mill.

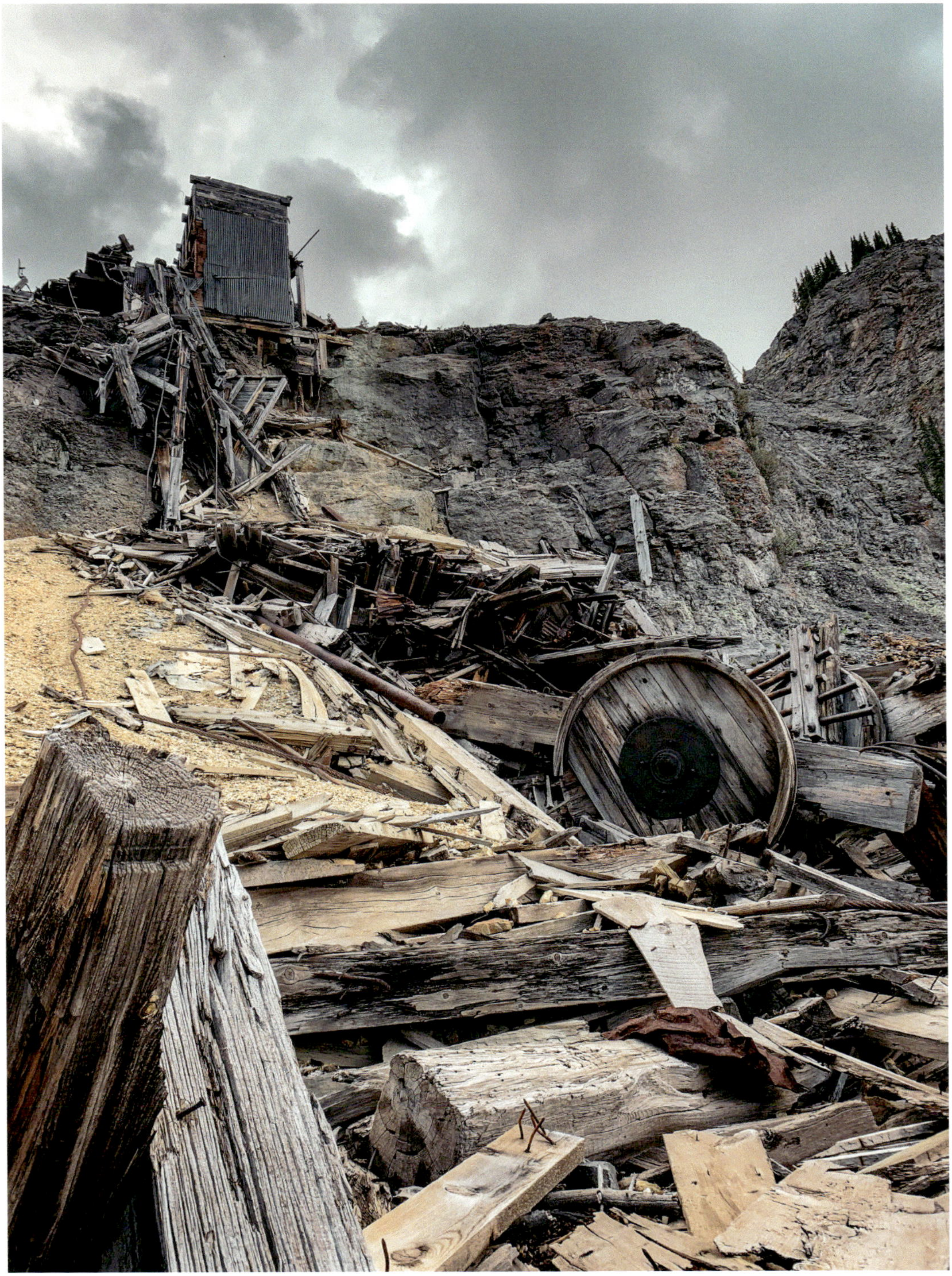

This crumbling mill above Telluride perfectly depicts the incredibly rugged terrain that miners in the area had to contend with.

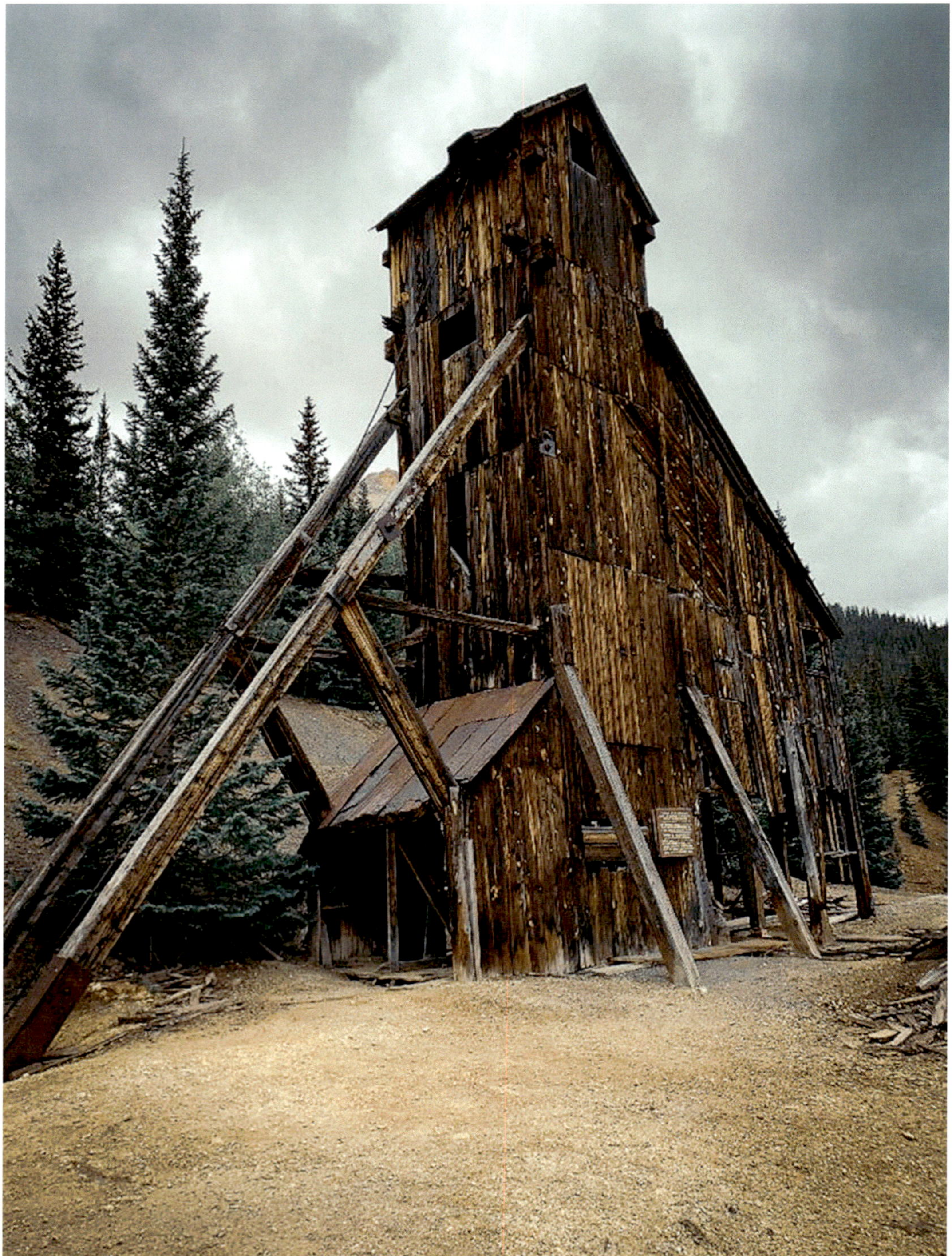

Shaft house of the Yankee Girl mine.

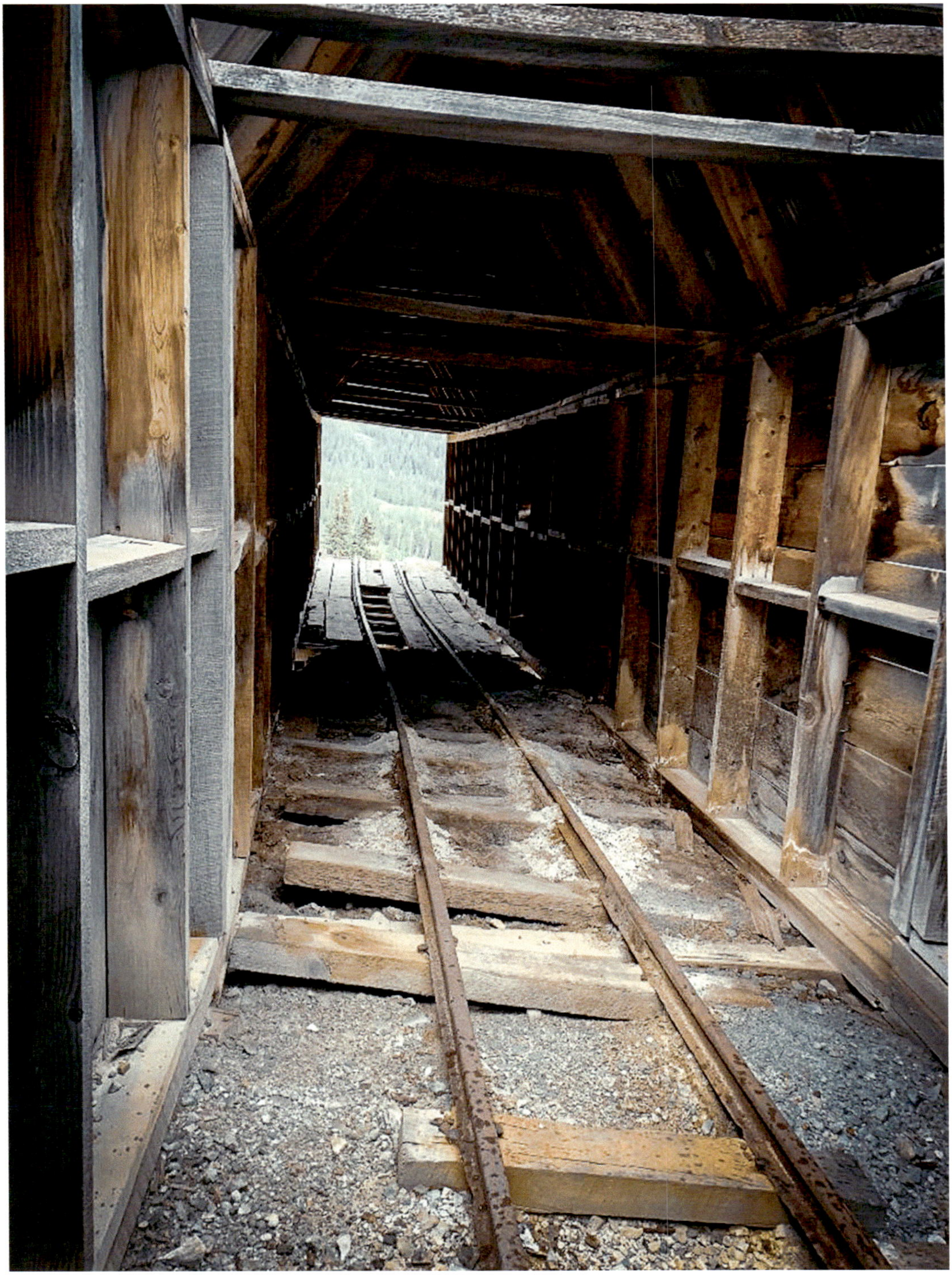

Ore cart tracks at the Genessee mine.

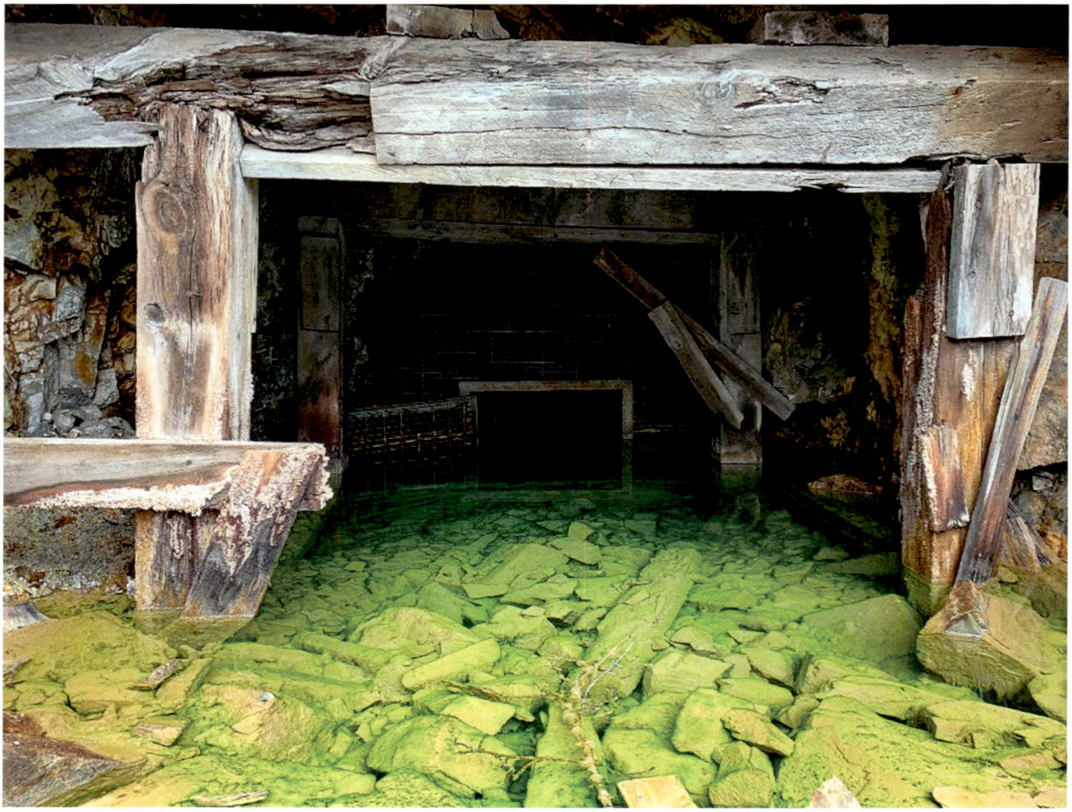

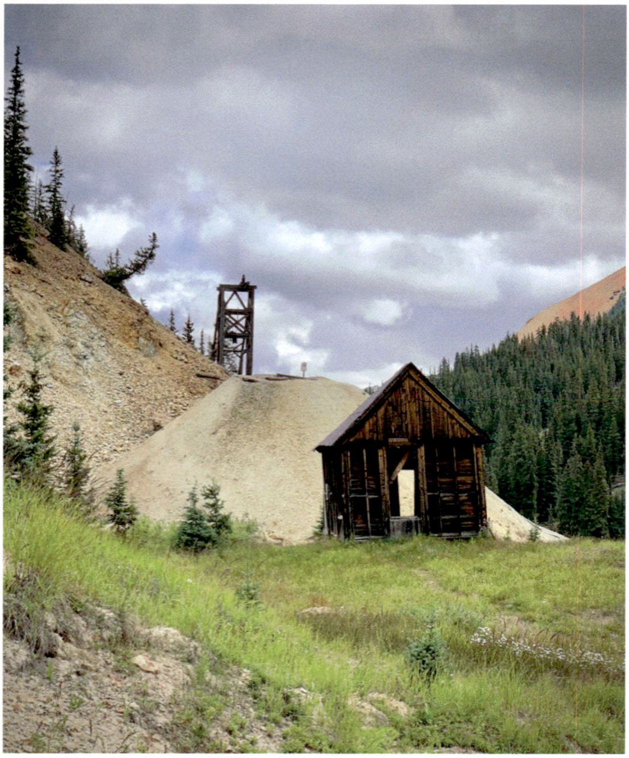

Above: Flooding was a major problem for the Red Mountain mines, as is depicted here at the Cora Belle mine.

Left: The headframe, a leaning cabin, and an old jailhouse are all that is left of the National Belle mine and the nearby Red Mountain Town.

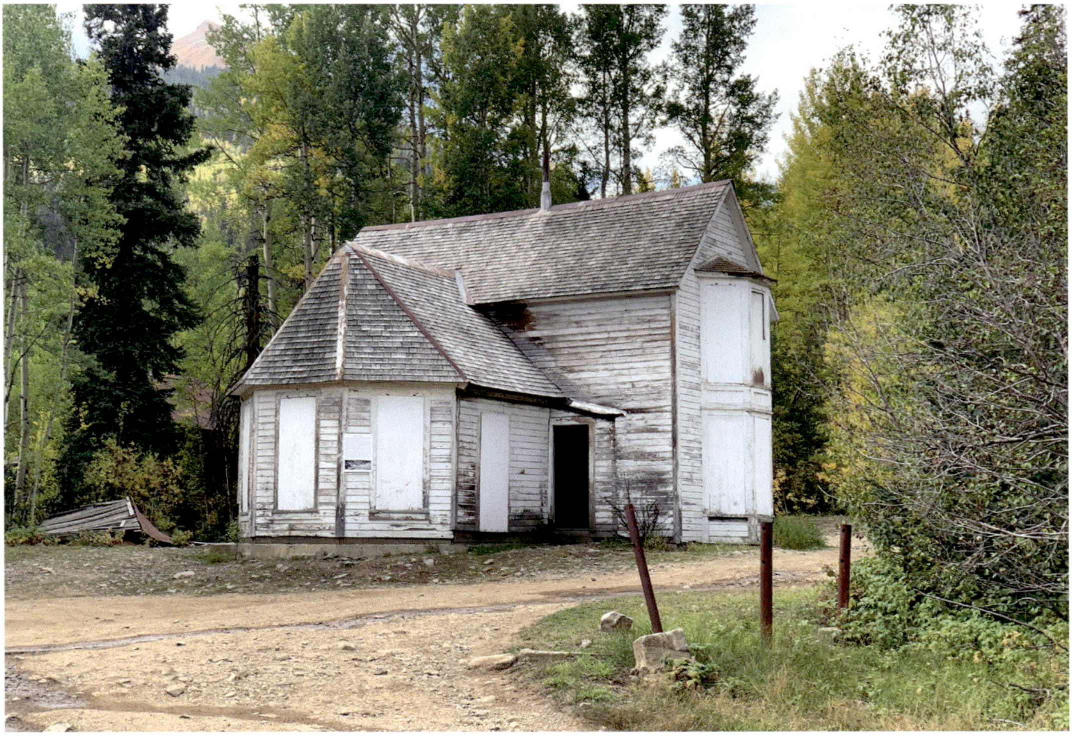

The Durgy-Allen house is the most prominent structure in the ghost town of Ironton, which was founded in 1883.

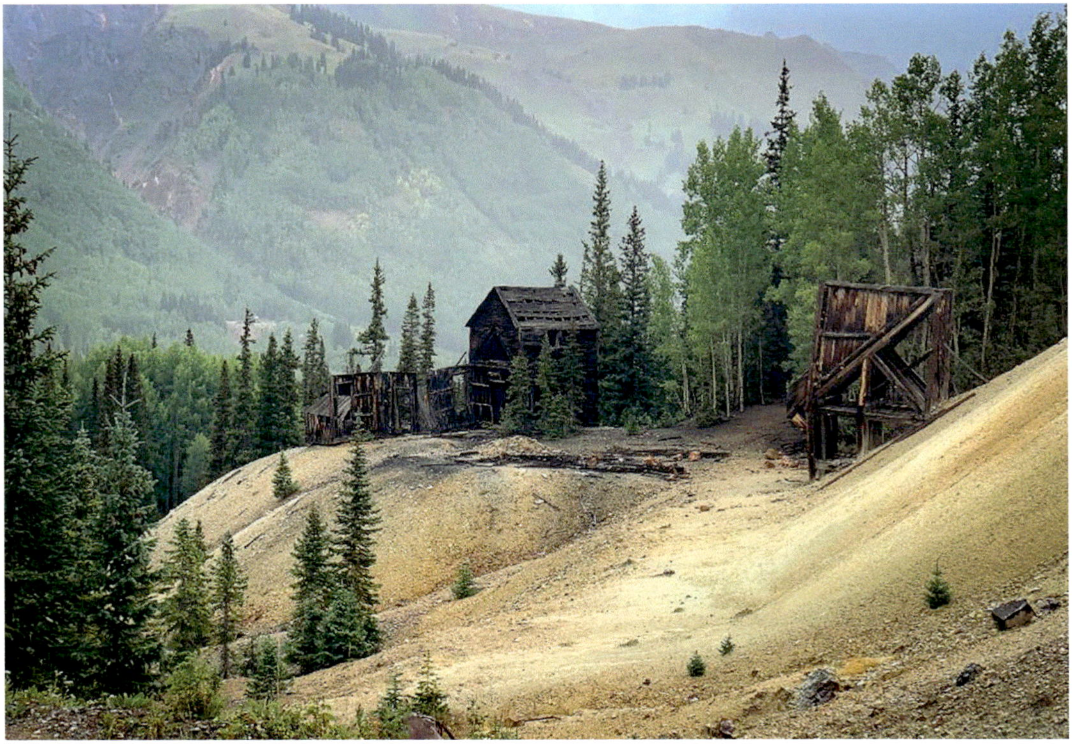

Outbuildings at the Guston-Robinson mine.

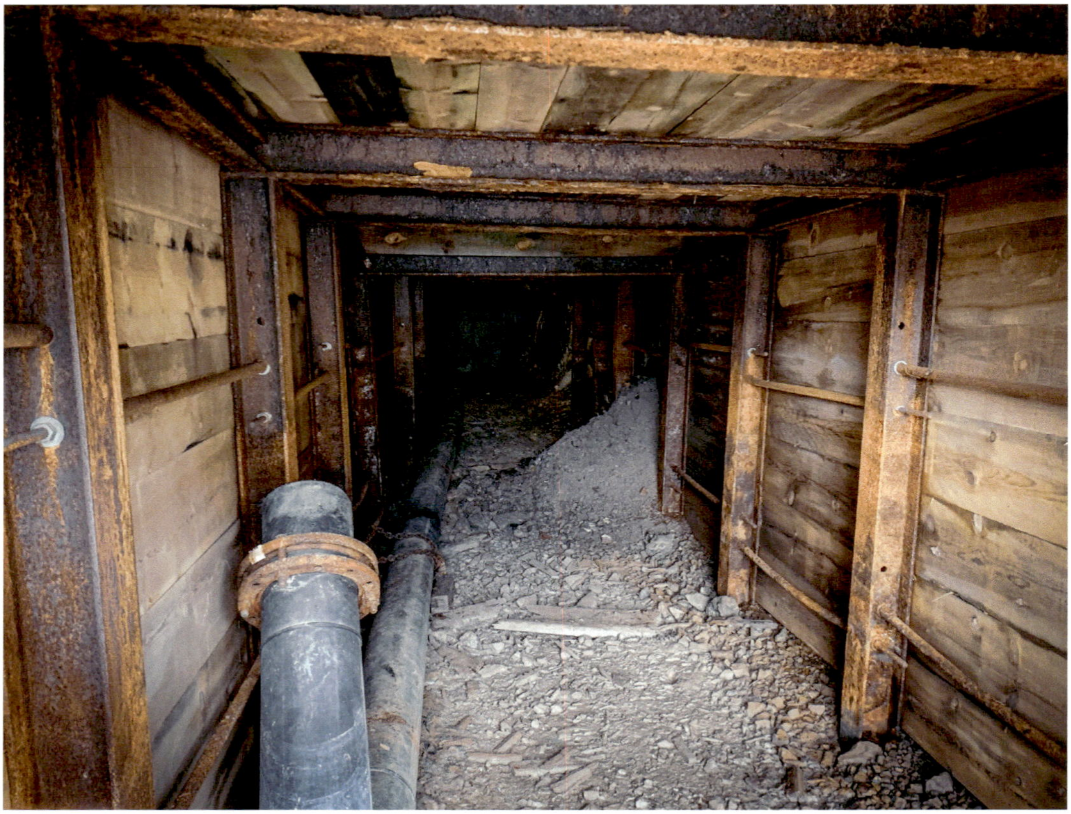

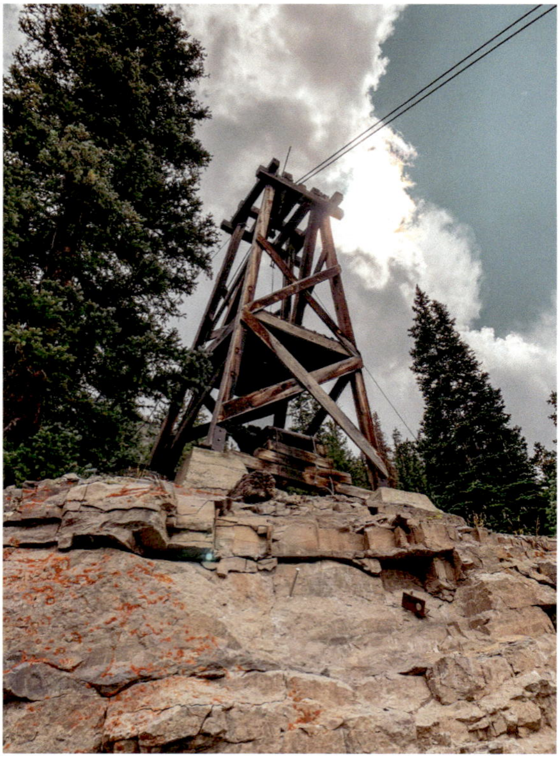

Above: Looking down the Bullion Tunnel, the main haulage adit for the Smuggler-Union mine.

Left: Cable tram systems like this one were a common method of transporting ore throughout the San Juan mining districts.

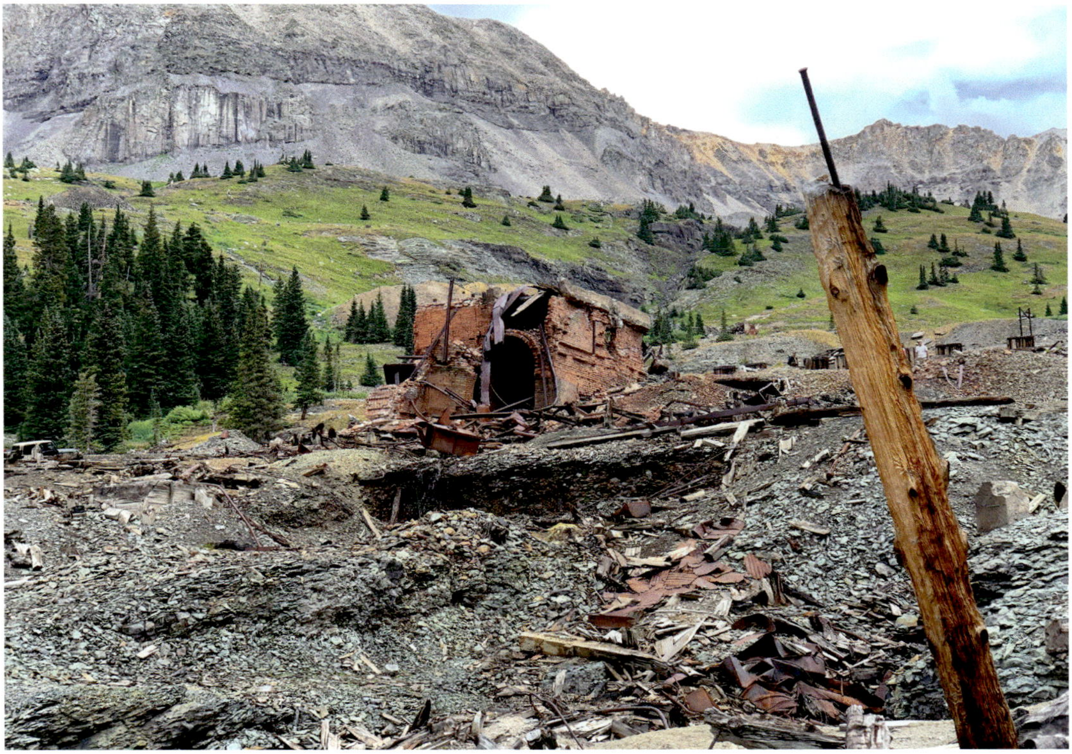

Tomboy townsite and mill.

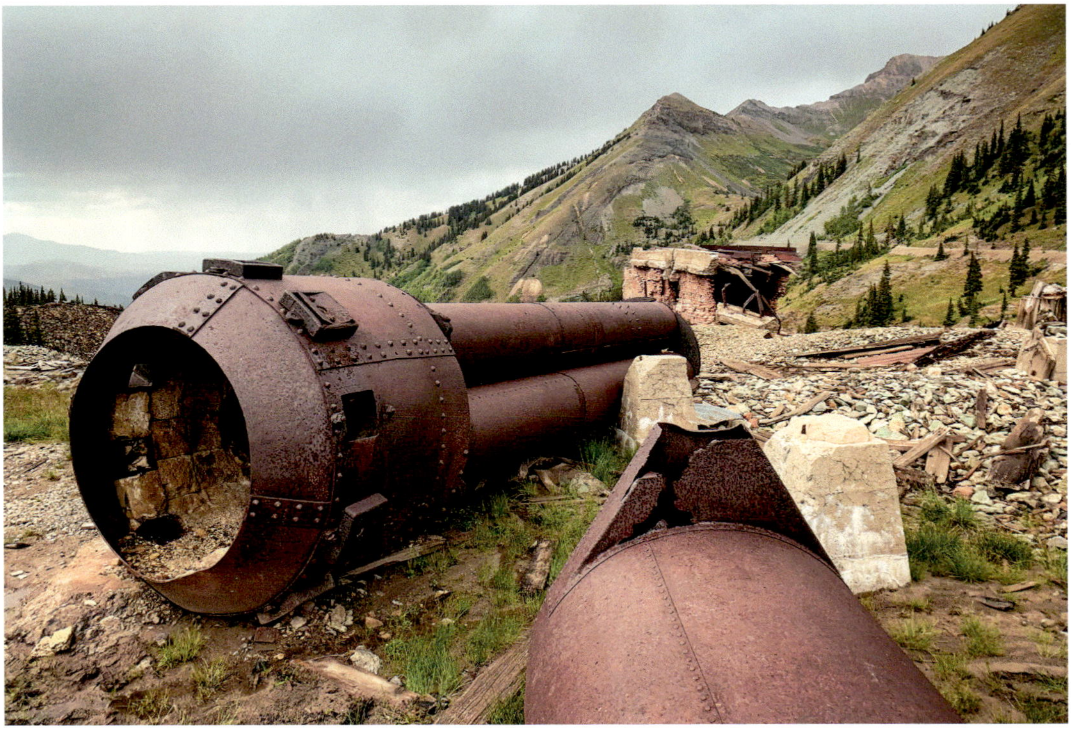

Not much left of the old Tomboy Mill.

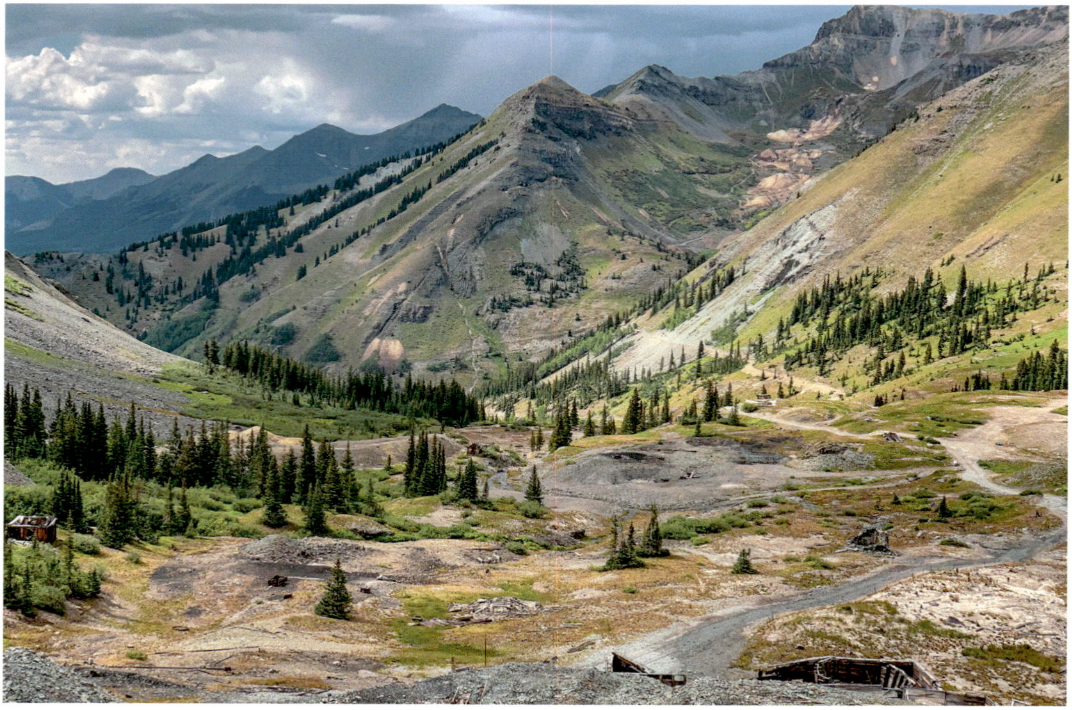

Looking towards the Smuggler-Union mine from the Tomboy townsite.

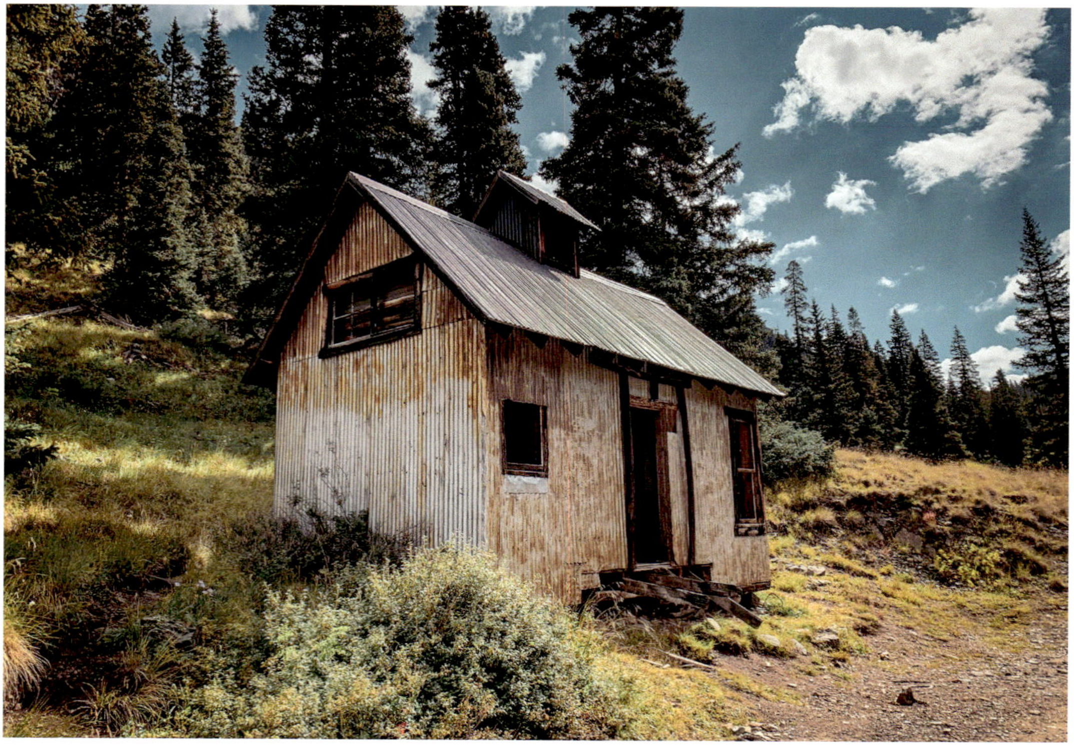

An old bunkhouse near Engineer Pass. Following the silver market crash, many mining camps in the San Juan Mountains were left abandoned.

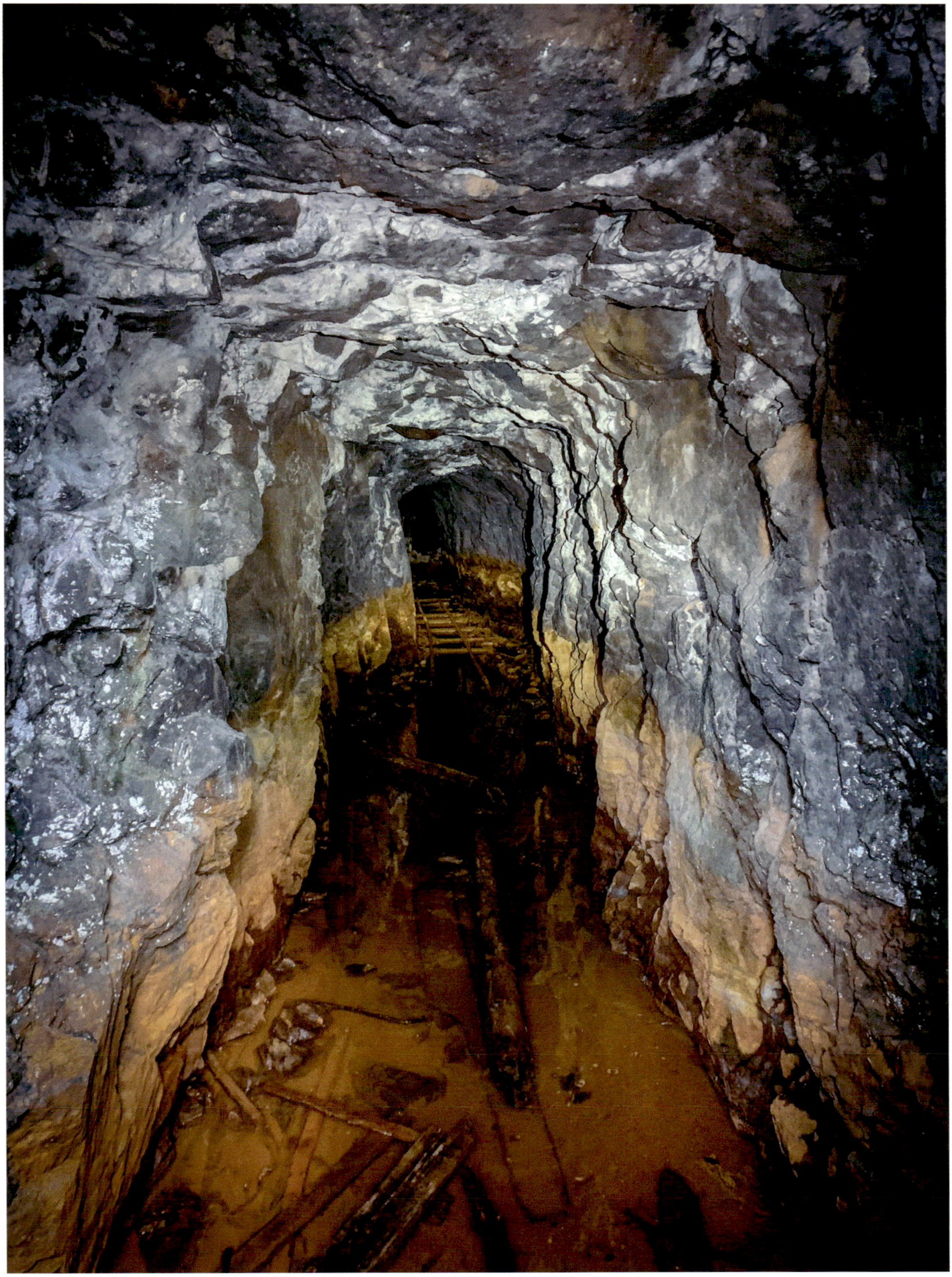

One of the countless mines idled after the silver market crashed in 1893.

4

BREAKING THE GILDED CAGE

While the silver market collapse was indisputably catastrophic, all was not lost for the Centennial State. The crash coincided fortuitously with the last great gold rush in Colorado's history.

In 1890, part-time prospector and full-time drinker "Crazy Bob" Womack claimed to have found gold in Poverty Gulch on the west face of Pikes Peak. No one believed him. Years earlier, three conmen had salted a nearby prospect hole with gold in an incident that became known as the Mount Pisgah Hoax. As such, the entire region had been written off by the mining community.

Incensed by the skepticism, the bibulous prospector hung a chunk of ore in the window of a furniture shop in Colorado City. The glistening rock caught the eye of a carpenter named Winfield S. Stratton. Intrigued, Stratton began his own exploration of the area, discovering the now-famous Independence lode in 1891. As for Womack, he sold his claim for a mere $300. It was later developed into the Gold King mine, which would go on to produce $5 million.

Hearing of Stratton's success, tens of thousands of prospectors flocked to Battle Mountain. Several towns boomed into existence, the largest being Cripple Creek. Starting as a haphazard tent city, the settlement rapidly grew into a proper town. By 1892, Cripple Creek had electricity, telephone, and telegraph lines. Saloons and brothels lined the streets, catering to the miners' every vice. Three railroads—the Midland Terminal Railway, the Colorado Springs and Cripple Creek Railway, and the Florence and Cripple Creek Railway—all laid tracks to the region, the latter winning the race in 1894.

When the silver market crashed, the gold-rich Cripple Creek District seemed to fare rather well. As the Colorado silver mines shut down, however, out-of-work miners began pouring in. With a surplus workforce available, many of the mine owners decided to lengthen the workday from eight to ten hours, with no increase in pay. Furious, the employees unionized, demanding the eight-hour day be reinstated at the original wage. When they were ignored, the union went on strike on February 7, 1894.

In an effort to break the strike, the mine owners called on El Paso County Sheriff Bowers to escort in scab workers. Twice he tried, but both times his deputies were driven out by an entrenched army of unionists, armed with rifles and dynamite. In response, the mining companies provided Bowers with enough capital to raise a veritable army, 1,200 men strong. Governor Davis H. Waite, a populist, sympathetic to the working man, quickly stepped in, declaring the mercenary force illegal and dispatching the state militia to intercept them. By the time the soldiers arrived, Bowers had lost control of his mercenary army, now running rogue through the streets, beating townspeople and miners alike. At the sight of Gatling guns and mounted militia, however, the paramilitary force quickly surrendered and disbanded. The mine owners were left with no choice but to give in to the union demands.

Emboldened by the victory, the Western Federation of Miners (W.F.M.) struck again in Leadville two years later. Here, they employed far more aggressive tactics. During the strike, fifty union men carried out a violent nighttime raid against four mines, attacking strikebreakers with dynamite and a homemade cannon. Again, the Colorado National Guard was called in. This time, however, the presence of the militiamen hamstrung the militant unionists, leading to the eventual failure of the strike.

A similar story played out in the town of Henson in 1899, which had a reputation for lawlessness, one blamed largely on its single, male, Italian population. Following a series of shootings, the Auric Mining Company declared that all unmarried men working the mines must move out of town and into company-owned boardinghouses. Rent was set high, and the conditions were deplorable.

Naturally, the decree did not sit well with the men who quietly began organizing a retaliation. In March, the state armory in Lake City was robbed of fifty rifles and several crates of ammunition. A few days later, 100 well-armed miners formed a picket line in front of the Ute-Ulay and the Hidden Treasure mines. They refused to let anyone pass until the housing policy was repealed.

Lake City Sheriff James Deck attempted to negotiate a peaceful resolution to the strike, but the unionists only became increasingly irate. Outgunned, he wired Governor Charles Thomas, petitioning him to send the state militia. Two days later, 300 soldiers arrived in Henson. With little chance of success, the miners surrendered. All who had taken up arms were fired and ordered to leave the county. An ad in the local paper called for replacement workers, specifying, "Italians need not apply."

In 1901, W.F.M. organized another strike at the Smuggler-Union mine, situated just above Telluride. The mine manager Arthur Collins had announced the implementation of the contract system. Also known as "fathoms," this old, Cornish wage model paid miners by the ore dug, not the work done. In such a system, ancillary but important safety work went unpaid and was therefore often neglected.

As with previous strikes, sheriff deputies were employed to protect a scab workforce. As the months dragged on, tensions reached a boiling point. In the dark and early hours of July 3, some three-hundred armed miners quietly took up positions around the heavily guarded Bullion Tunnel. A committee of twenty-five union men walked out of the darkness and approached the mine. When they were blocked by the sentries, one of the men shouted towards the bunkhouse, demanding that the strikebreakers leave at once. Before he got the words out, a deputy pulled a pistol and shot him through the throat. The hillsides erupted in gunfire, igniting a violent gun battle. The seven-hour fight left three men dead and ten wounded.

When it was all over, the union had taken control of the mine. They rounded up the strikebreakers and marched them over Imogene Pass, threatening to kill them should they ever return. With his mine shut down, Collins had little choice but to give in to the union demands. He was later murdered in his home following a deadly fire that was blamed on cut-rate safety measures.

The insurgent federation was rapidly becoming a major threat to the capitalists of Colorado. Twice, they had forcibly bent mine companies to their will, and now, nearly every trade in Cripple Creek had unionized. The town was emerging as the center of a new, socialist movement—one capable of wielding great economic power over a state that was dependent on mining.

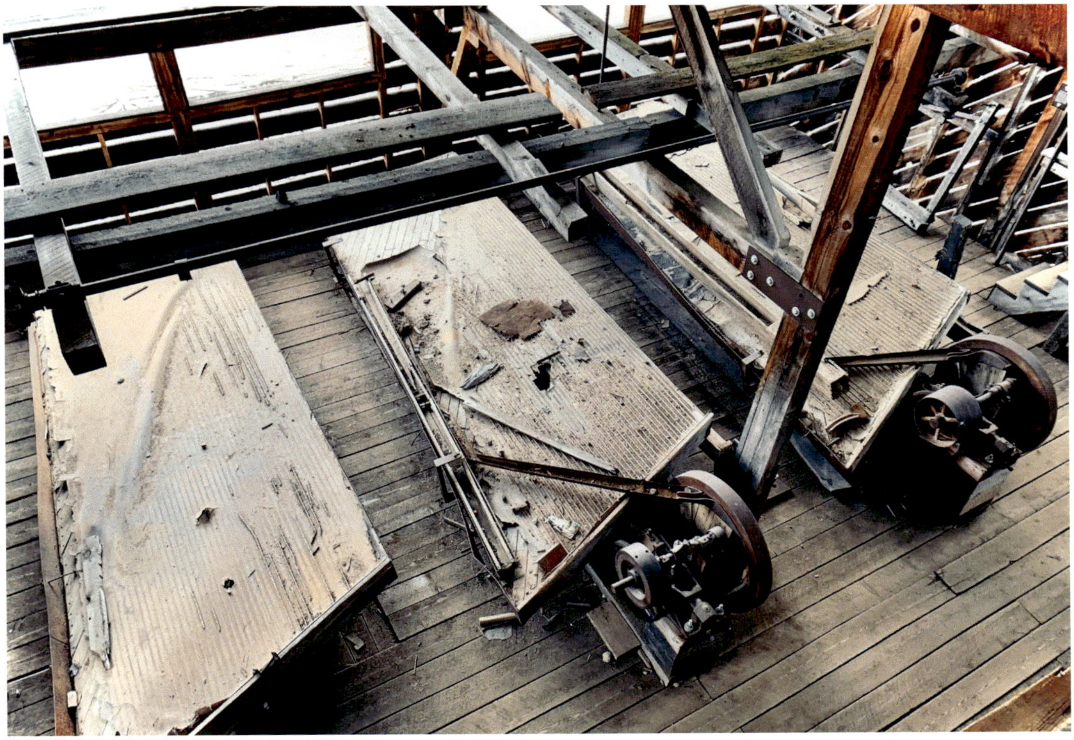

Wilfley tables inside the Sound Democrat Mill, which was shuttered largely due to a second economic panic in 1907.

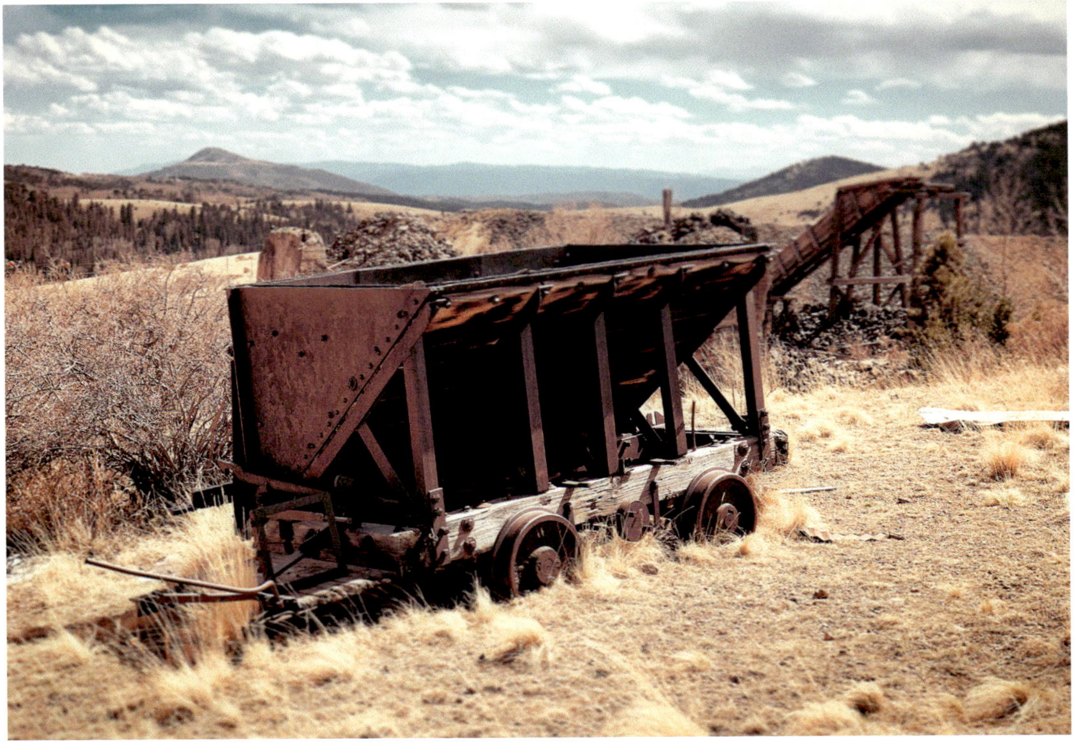

A side-dump ore cart sits outside the Independence mine, the claim that put Cripple Creek on the map.

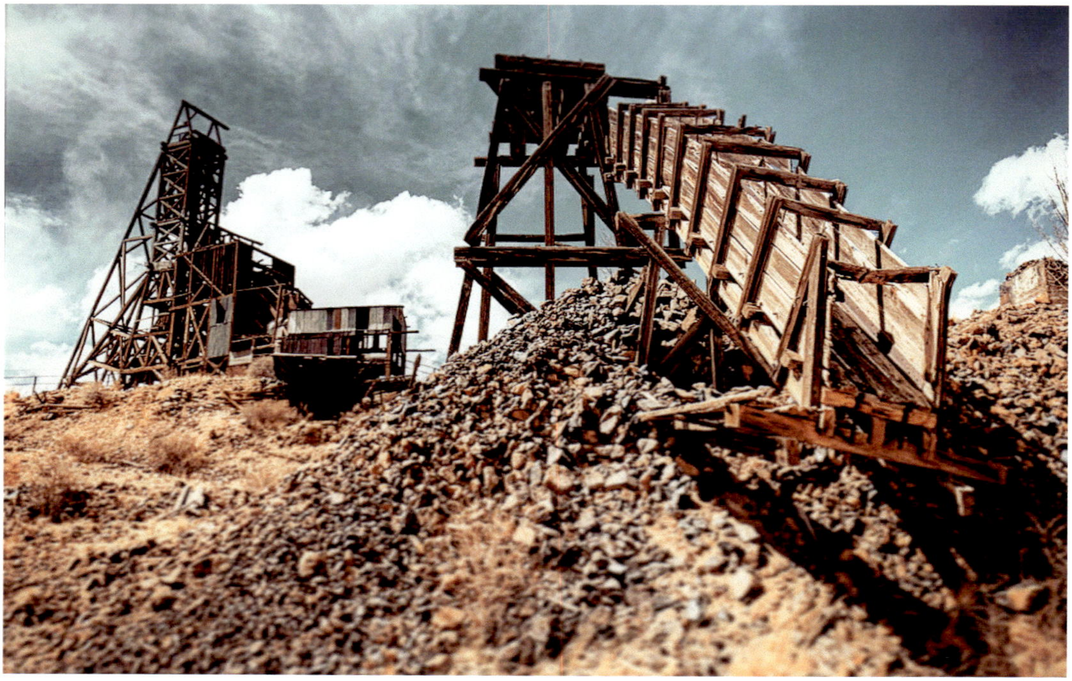

An ore chute descends from Stratton's famed Independence mine.

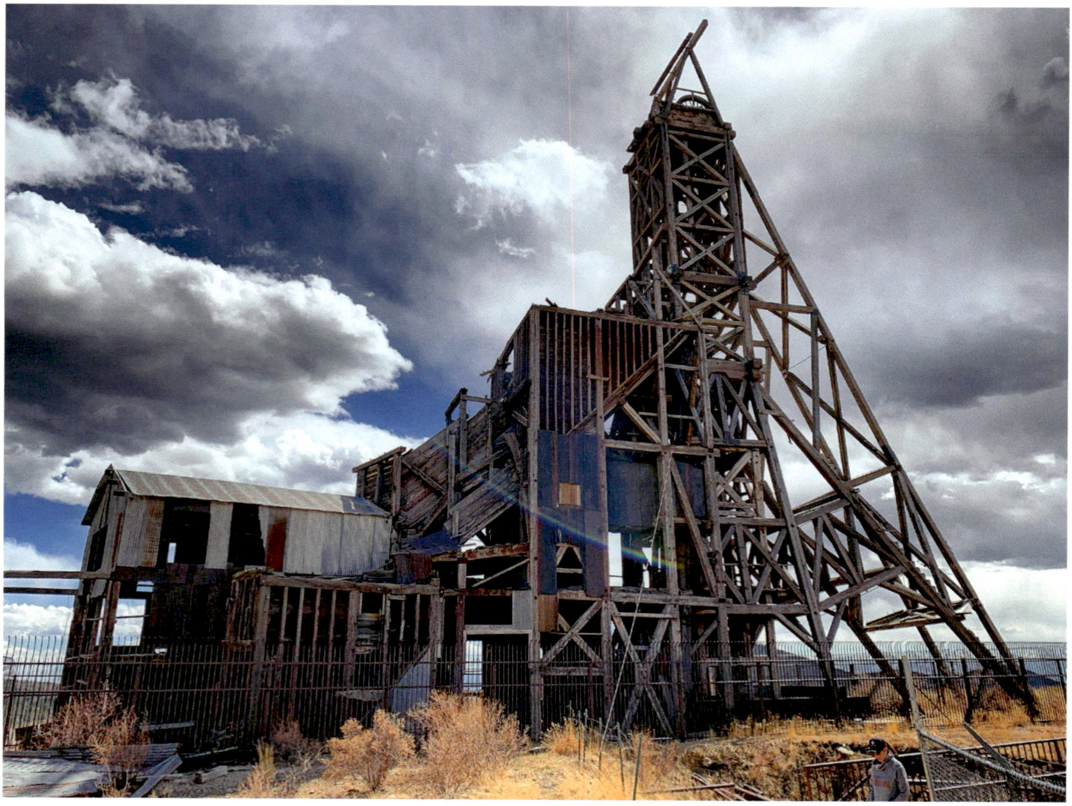

Headframe of the Independence mine.

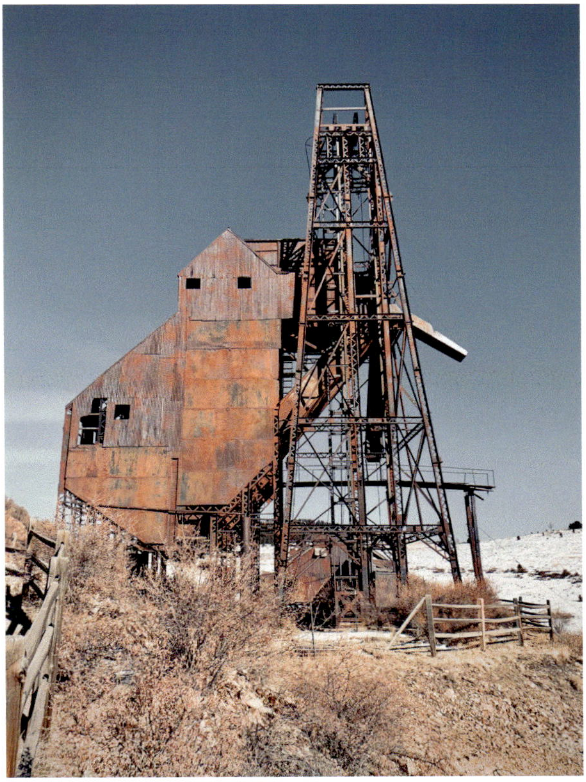

The Theresa mine began operation in 1895, just north of Stratton's claim. During a period of abandonment in the 1920s, it was nearly swallowed up by the enormous tailings pile being generated by the nearby Vindicator mine.

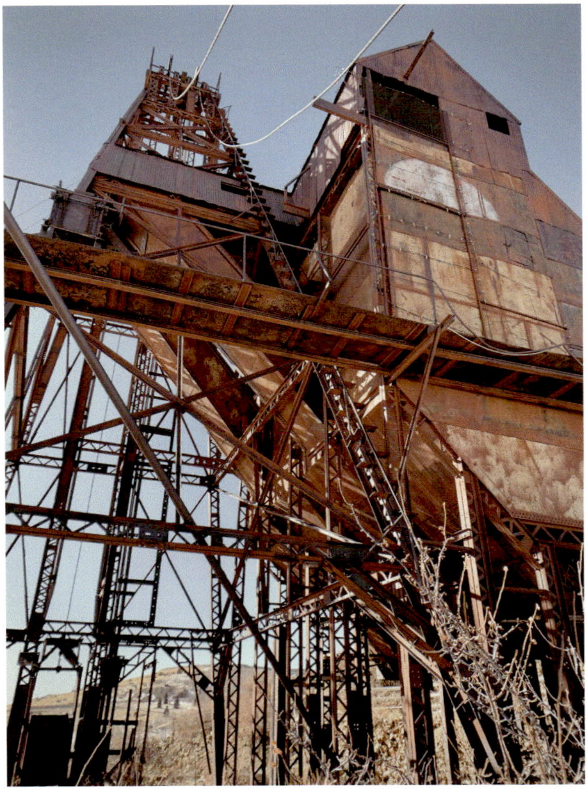

In 1934, a fire destroyed the surface plant of the Theresa mine. A new, steel headframe was constructed with an integrated orehouse. The colossal structure has become a historical icon of the area.

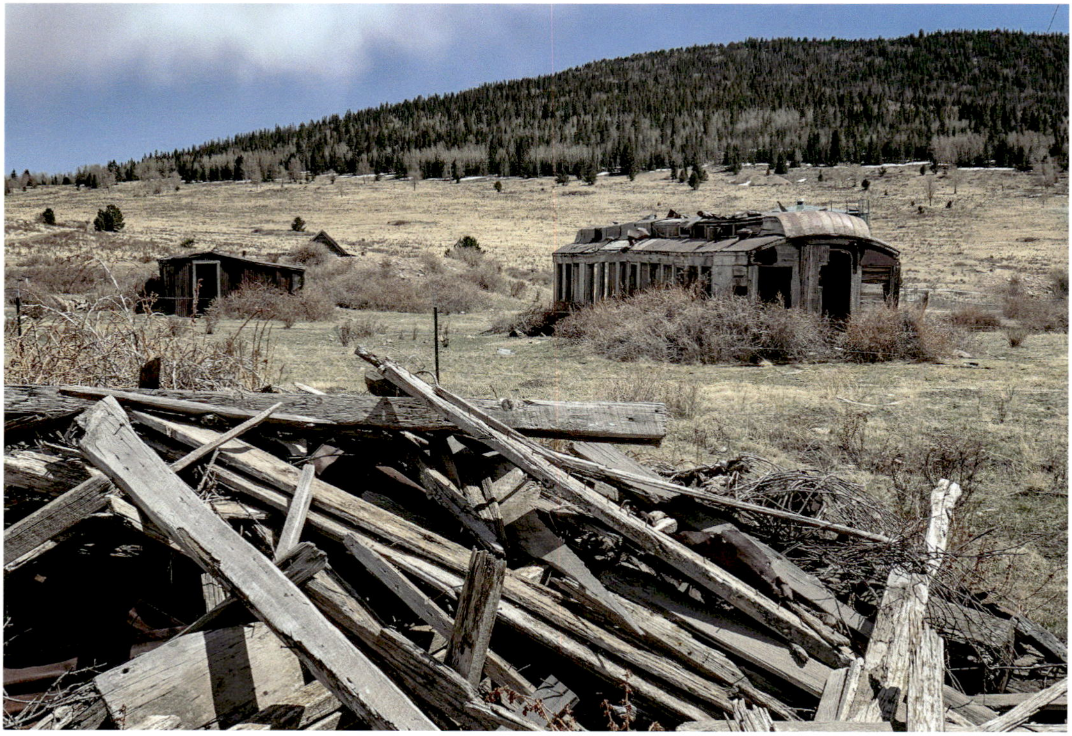

Crumbling structures and a forgotten passenger car mark the townsite of Altman.

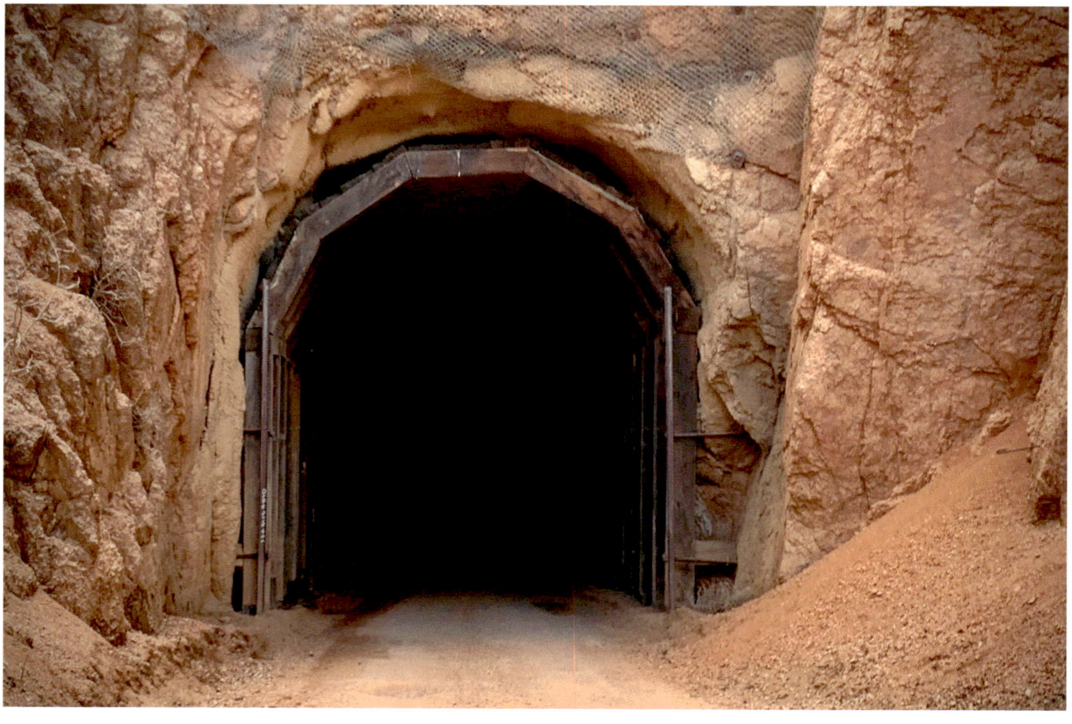

One of the many tunnels along Gold Camp Road, an old railroad grade snaking from Cripple Creek to Colorado Springs.

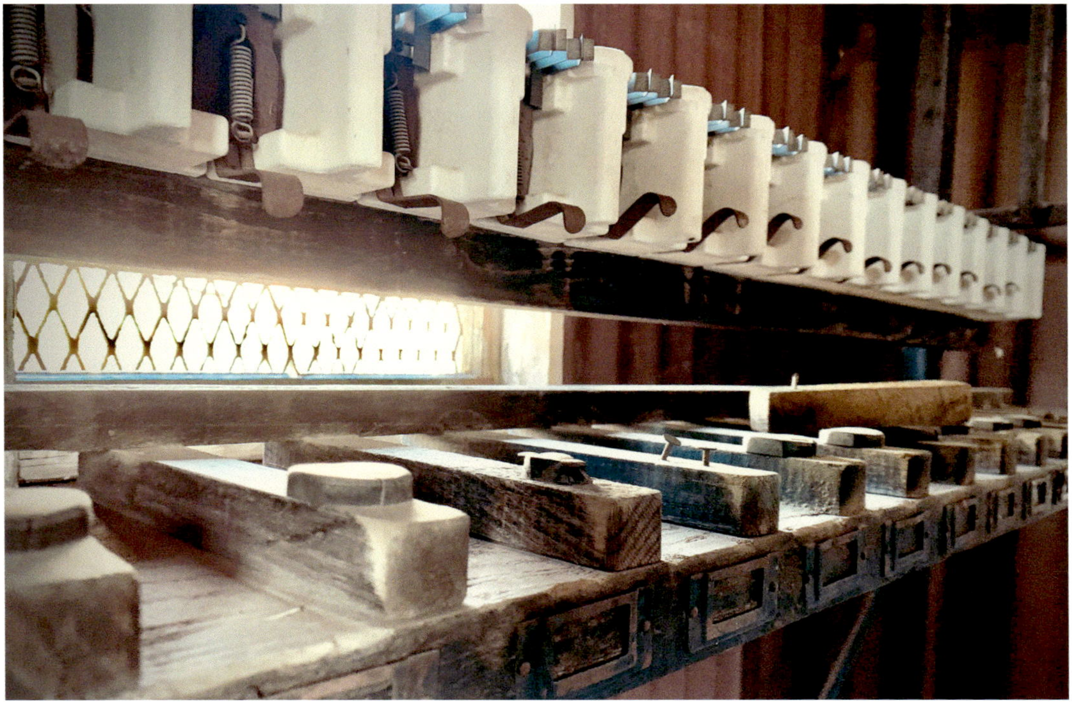

Electric and battery-powered lights replaced carbide lamps in the early 1900s. The nickel-iron batteries were recharged at the end of each shift on labeled racks like this one at the Theresa mine.

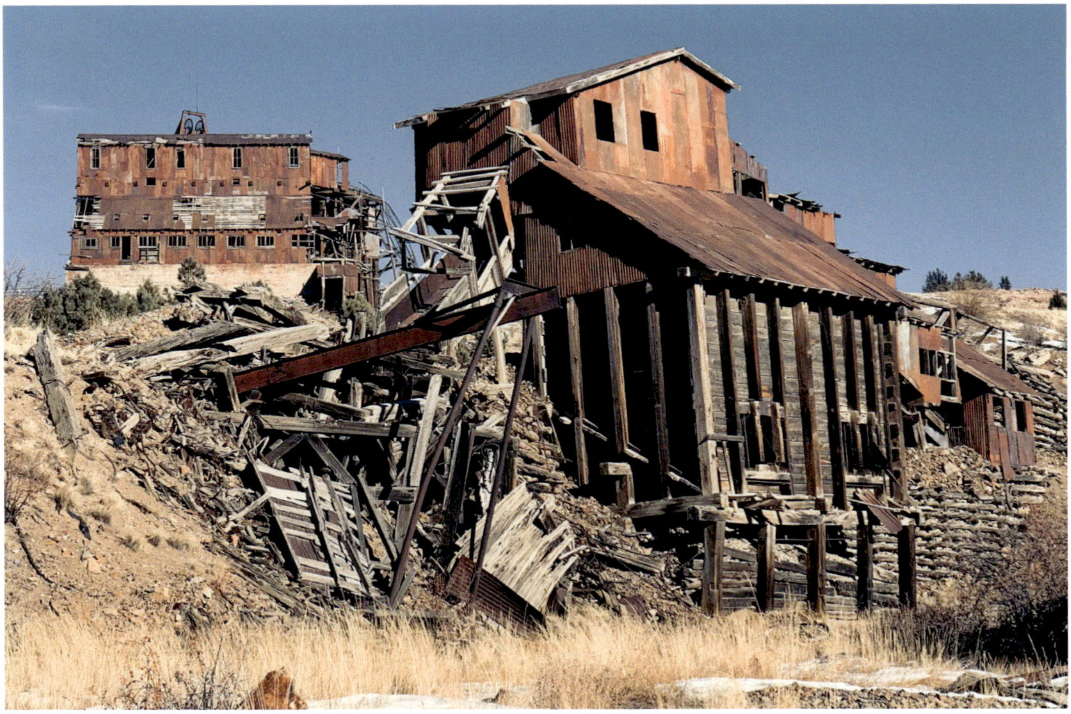

The Cripple Creek district enjoyed immense success well into the twentieth century. Much of the mining infrastructure can still be seen today.

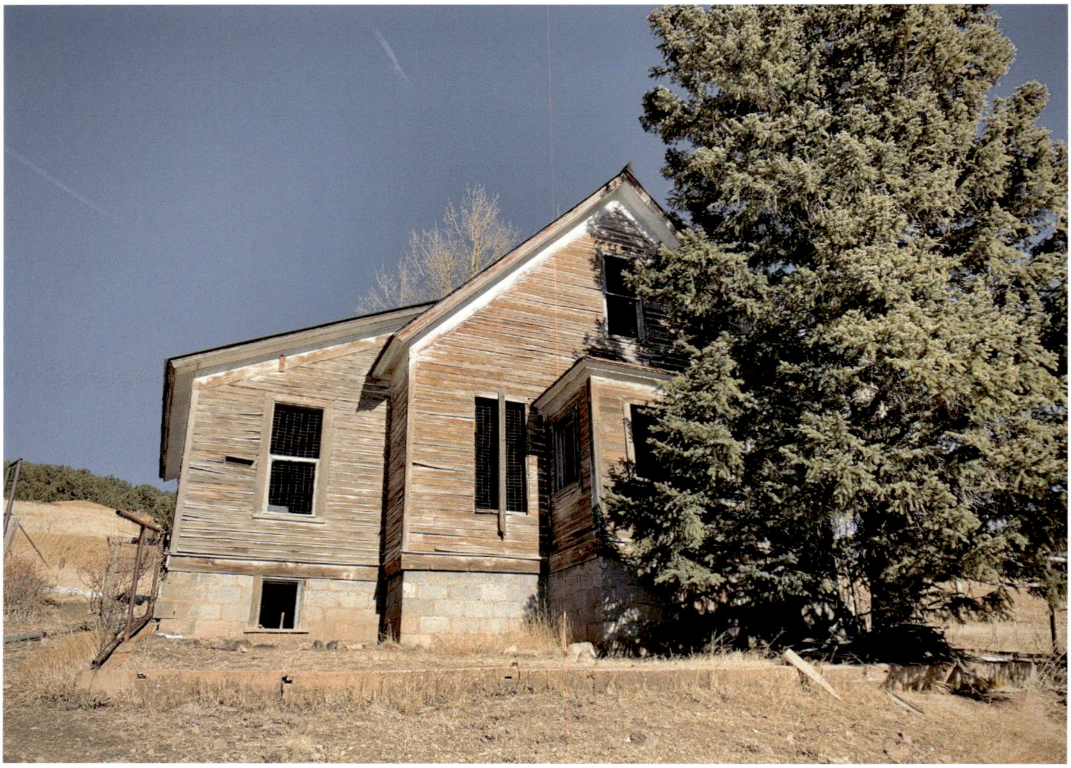

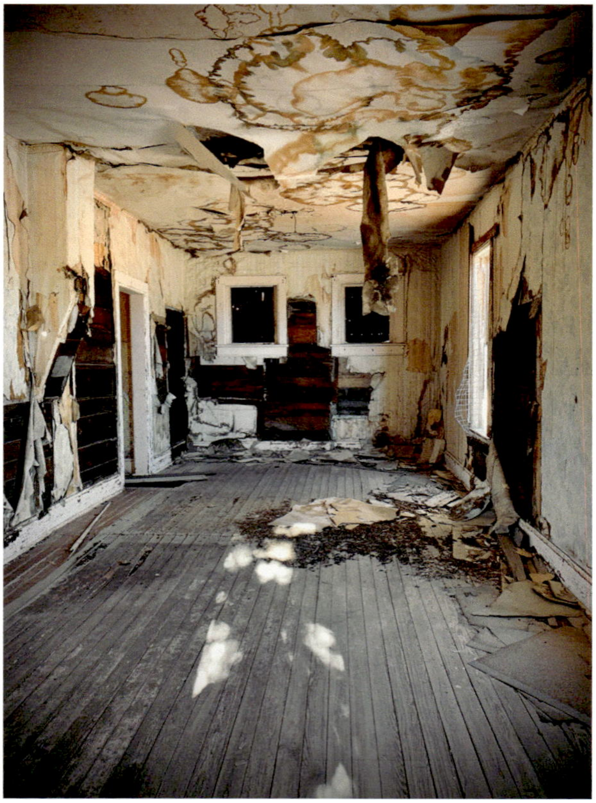

Above: The success and longevity of the region can be seen in the structures that remain. This weathered Victorian home, located in Independence, is downright palatial compared to the stacked-log cabins seen in most bygone mining towns.

Left: The parlor of a derelict home in Independence.

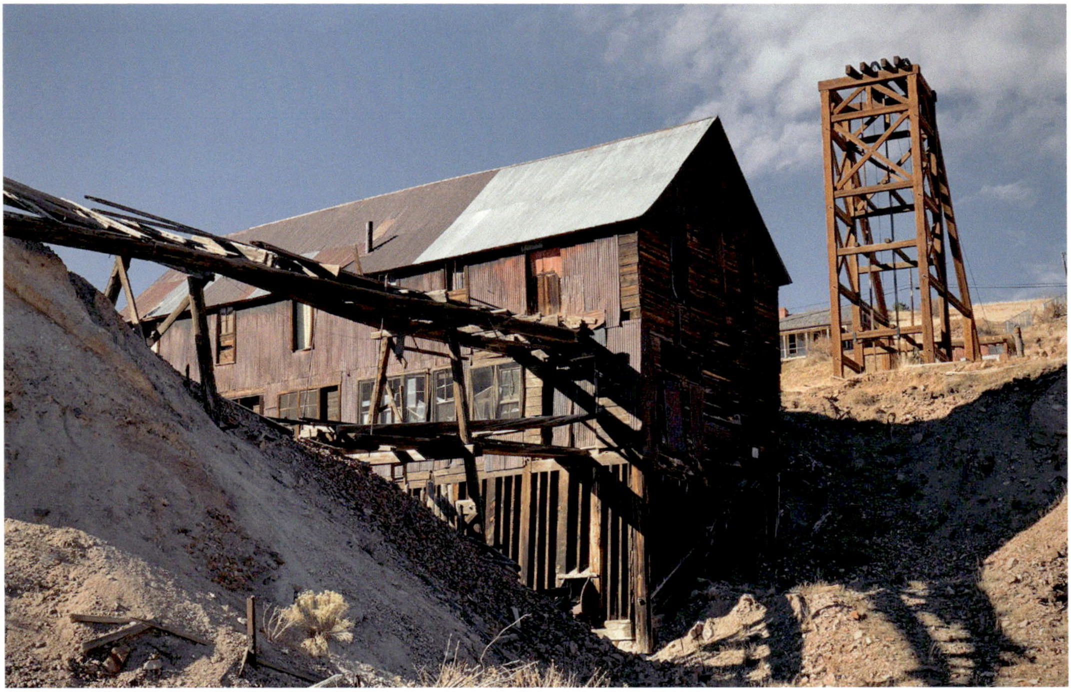

Some 125 deputies were forced to retreat after strikers dynamited the shaft house and boiler at the Strong mine (shown here), showering the men with shrapnel.

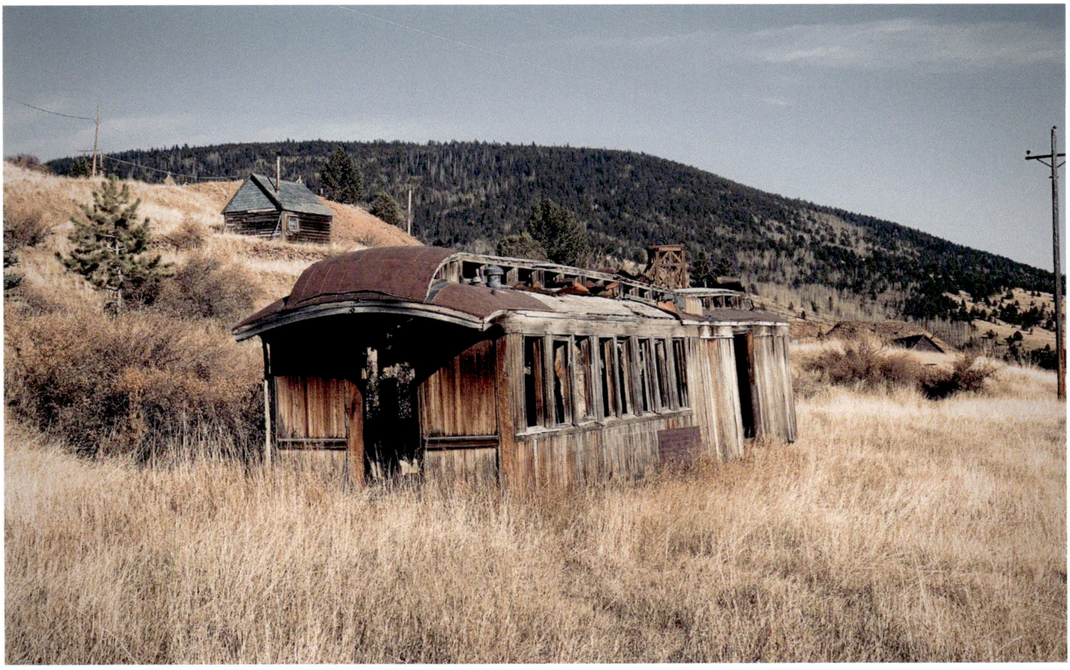

An old rail car sits near the defunct Victor depot. Following their victory against the first wave of deputies, a group of intoxicated miners loaded a train car with dynamite and attempted to roll it into the lawmens' camp. When this failed, they commandeered a locomotive and charged into Victor, guns blazing. The frivolous sortie cost the lives of one miner and one deputy.

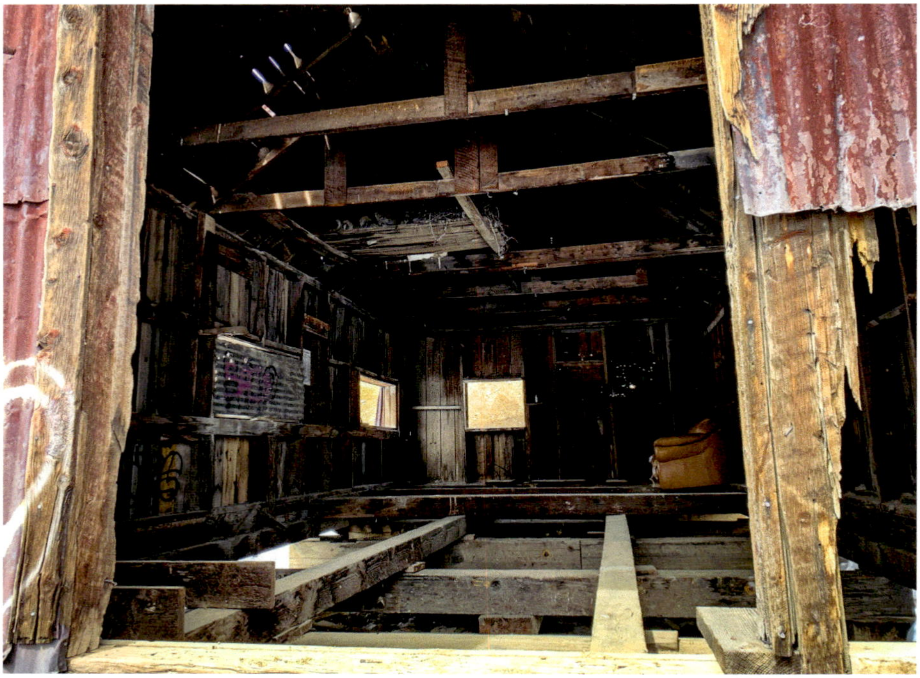

Interior of the Emmett mine boardinghouse. W.F.M. strikers used a homemade cannon to blow a hole in the defensive wall that surrounded this mine and attempted to dynamite the shaft house. They were forced to withdraw after strikebreakers cut down one of their men.

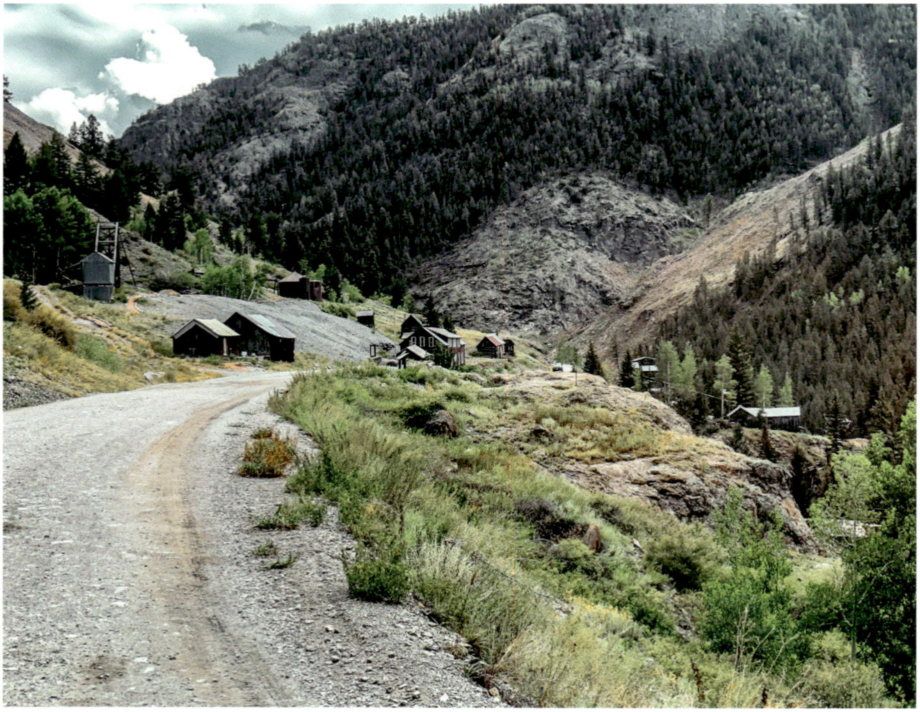

The ghost town and mining complex of Henson. Minerals were first discovered here in 1871, two years before the Brunot Treaty was signed.

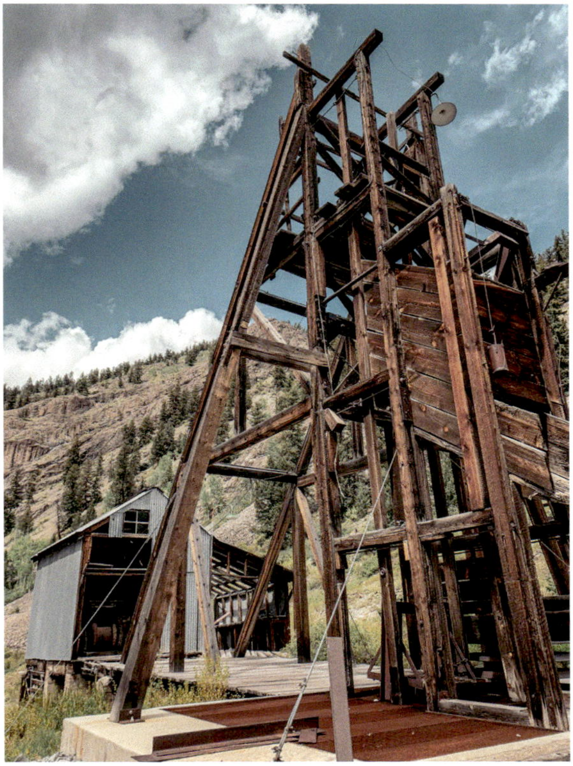

Right: Headframe of the Ute-Ulay mine.

Below: Water and fuel tanks at the Ute-Ulay mine display a rather threatening warning.

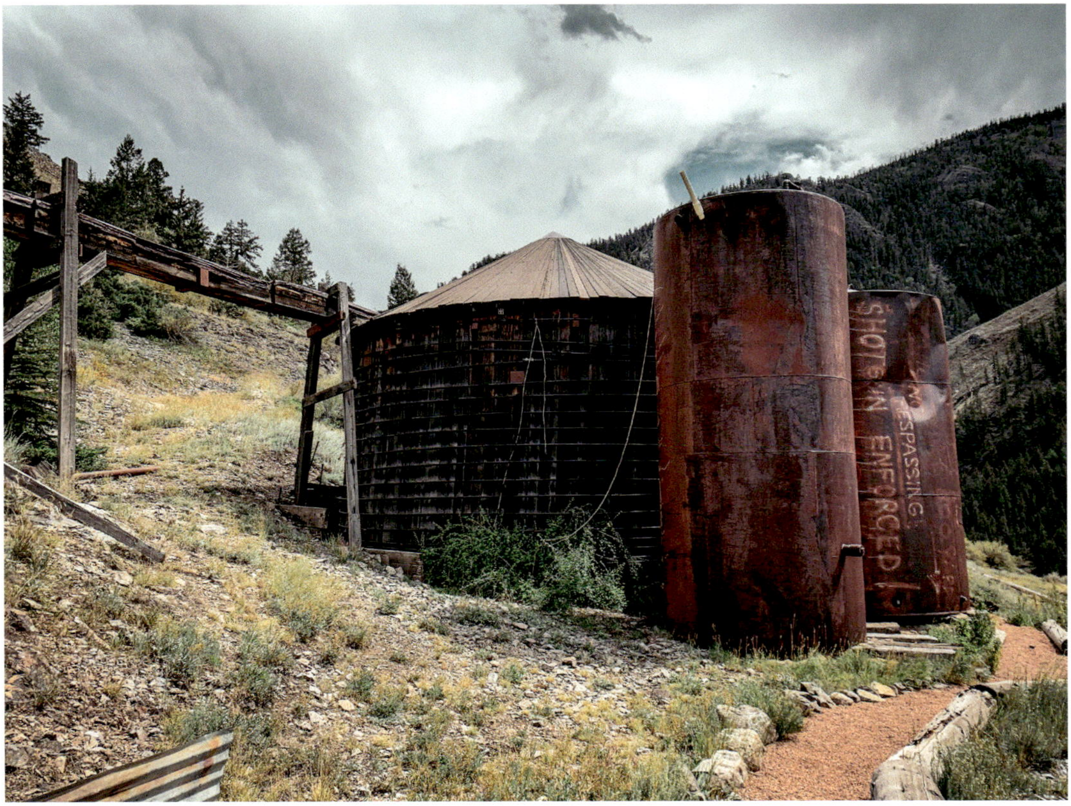

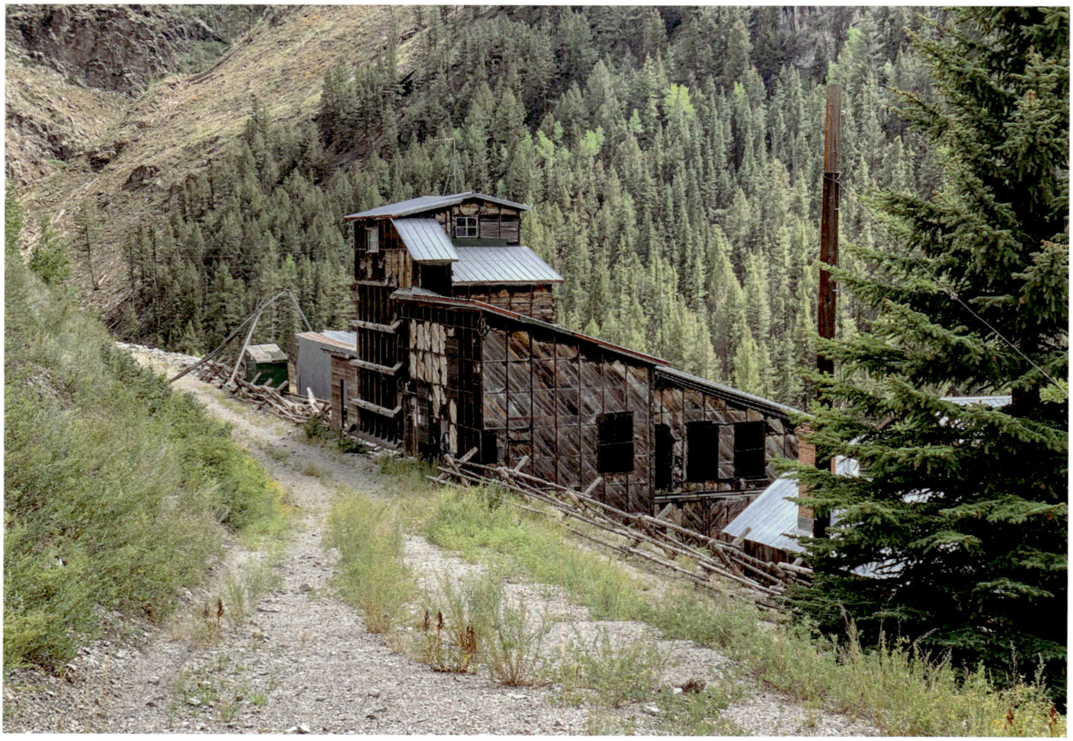

This mill was built in the 1930s and was in use as late as 1983.

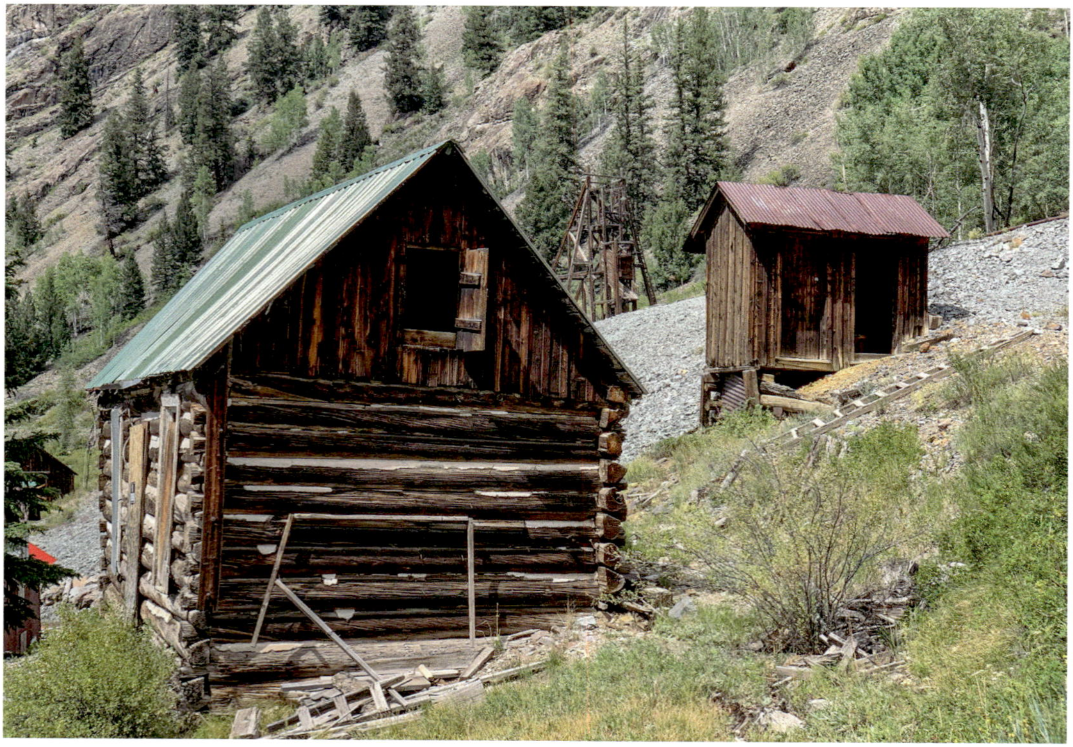

A dozen or so structures remain standing in the town of Henson, some dating back to the 1800s.

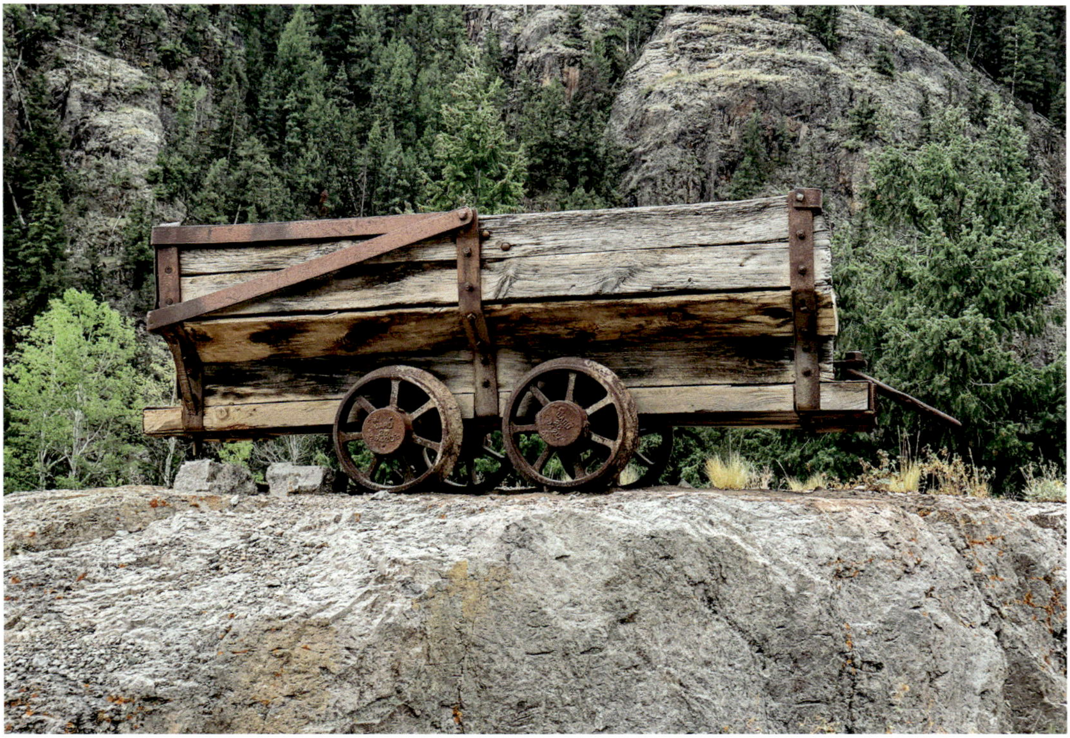

A rare, wooden ore cart from the Ute-Ulay mine.

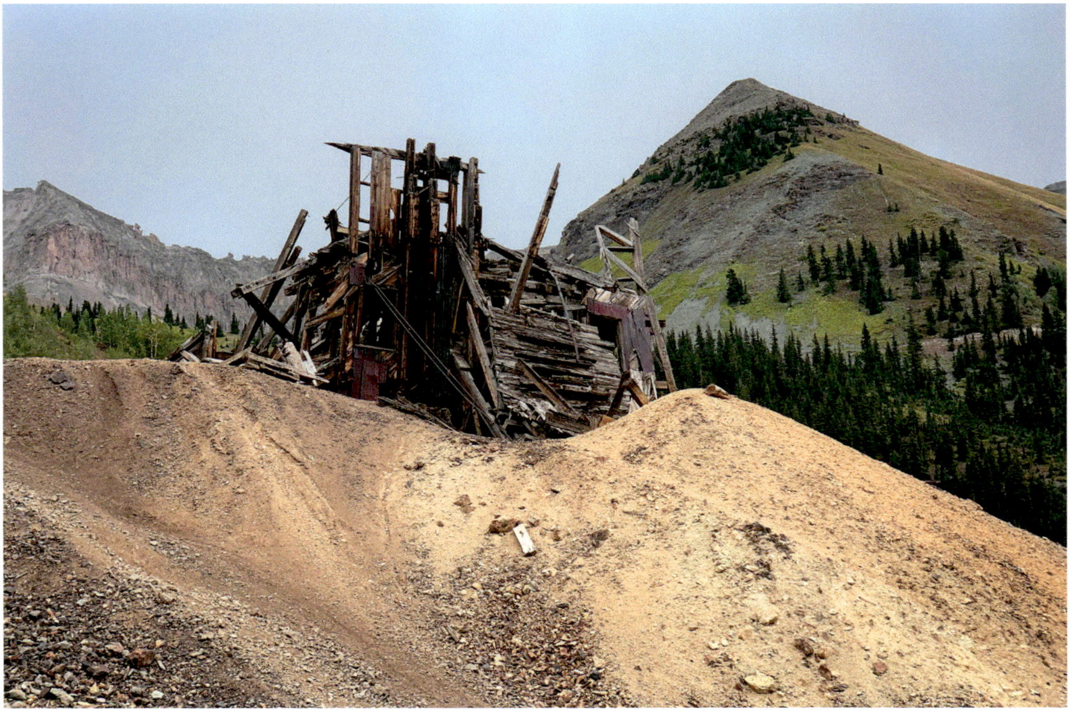

Once the crown jewel of the Telluride mining scene, the Smuggler-Union's considerable infrastructure has been reduced to heaps of timbers.

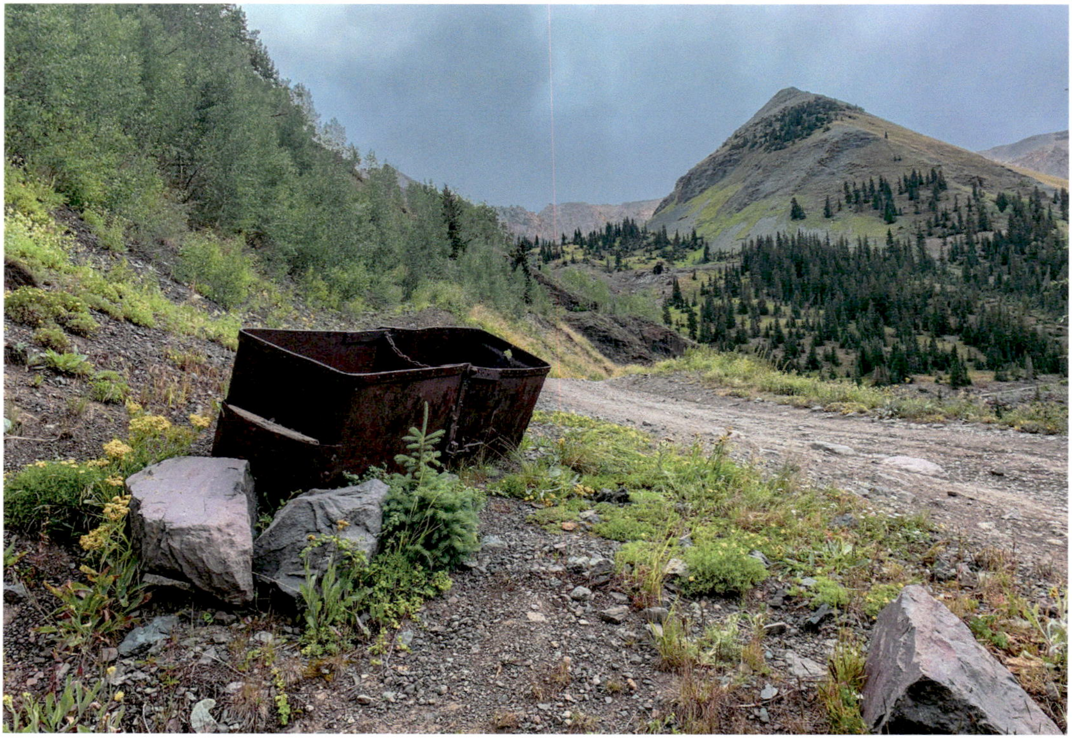

A rusting ore bin sits outside the Smuggler-Union mine.

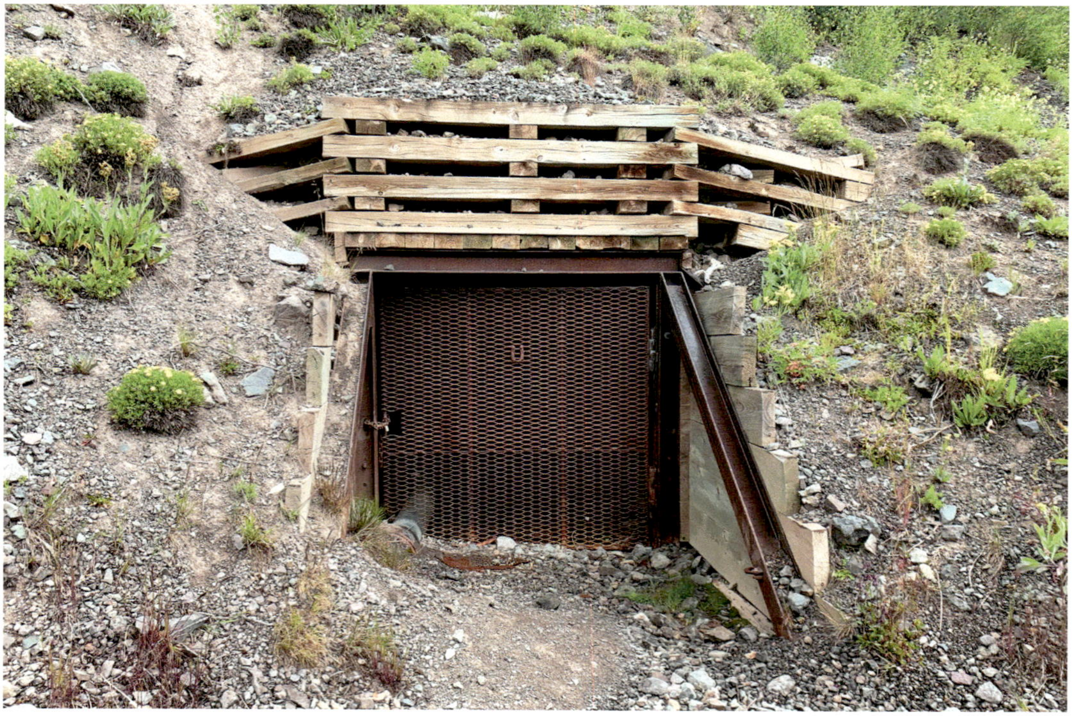

The Bullion Tunnel was the main haulage adit for the Smuggler-Union. During the battle with the unionists, strikebreakers were forced to retreat into the drift to escape the hail of bullets.

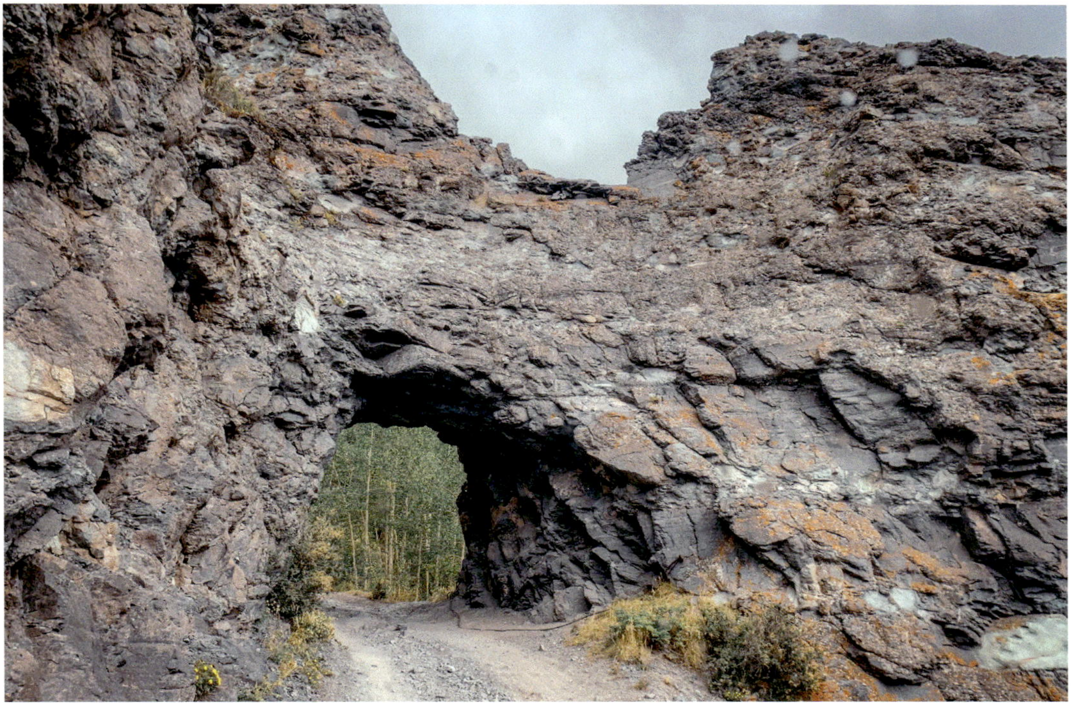

Known as the "Social Tunnel," this rock arch was a popular meeting place for miners and prostitutes. During the riot, W.F.M. strikers utilized it as a natural chokepoint to bar anyone from reaching the mine.

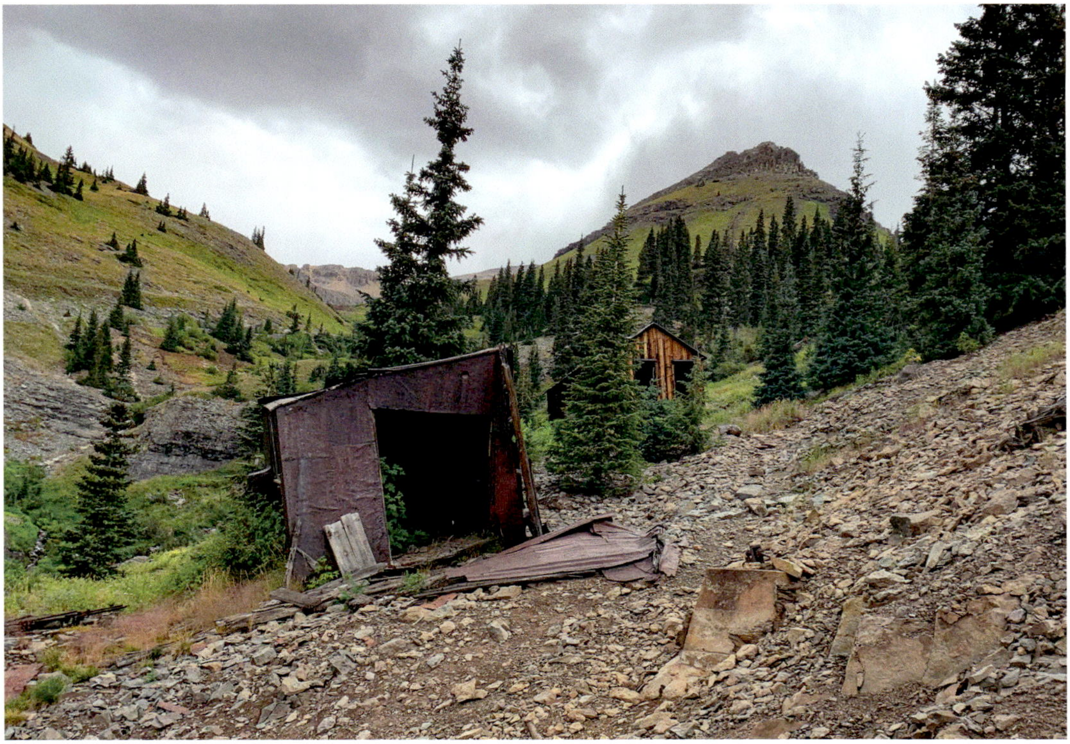

A few shacks still stand in the company town of Smuggler.

5

COLORADO LABOR WARS

It is worth mentioning here that not every mine in Colorado participated in the labor unrest. In the San Juan Mountains, mining had resumed after an Irish immigrant named Thomas Walsh discovered gold in Imogene Basin. Walsh's mine, known as Camp Bird, quickly grew to become one of the most successful operations in the world. At least part of this success can be attributed to Walsh's philanthropic nature. Workers at Camp Bird were treated to fair wages, an eight-hour workday, and accommodations comparable to most respectable hotels of the time. Unfortunately, Walsh's operation was an anomaly in this manner, and many Colorado miners felt they deserved similar treatment.

In 1903, the W.F.M. launched a series of strikes all across Colorado. Workers walked out in Idaho Springs, Denver, Durango, Cripple Creek, Colorado City, and Telluride. This time, they demanded the eight-hour day be extended to mill workers, many of whom were serving twelve-hour shifts. In a show of force, the union shut down every mine in Cripple Creek, most of which were not shipping ore to the offending mills, and played no part in the matter. Some strikers again resorted to violence. Union mobs brutally attacked strikebreakers, blew up buildings, and sabotaged mining equipment.

Yet the W.F.M. lacked a key component that had made previous strikes a success—a sympathetic governor. With the help of the state's most powerful businessmen, newly elected Republican James Peabody aimed to crush the unions once and for all. Colorado National Guard troops were dispatched to Cripple Creek and Telluride with orders to break the strike. Under the command of General Sherman Bell, the militia stripped union men of their guns and imprisoned them for "talking too much;" pro-union newspapers were shut down and reporters arrested; and even children were thrown into the stockade for taunting soldiers. Prisoners who demanded a trial were accompanied into the courtroom by armed guardsmen while Gatling guns were trained on the courthouse. Unfazed by the intimidation tactics, the judge consistently ruled in favor of the defendants. Bell, however, refused to release the prisoners until Governor Peabody ordered him to do so.

In order to further disrupt the W.F.M., the Baldwin-Felts and Pinkerton detective agencies were hired to infiltrate and sabotage the union's efforts. In November, a bomb, jerry-rigged to a guardrail inside the Vindicator mine, exploded, killing two employees. Albert Horsley (a.k.a. Harry Orchard) claimed responsibility for the blast, saying the W.F.M. hired him to do it. Orchard was a notoriously unscrupulous character, later admitting he had been in Pinkerton's employee.

Soon after, railroad spikes were discovered missing in a plot to derail a train full of strikebreakers. Earlier that same day, a detective hired by the mine owners had asked a railroad engineer where the worst place for a derailment would be. Curiously, it was the exact location the engineer pointed out to the detective where he would later find the missing spikes. The union was again blamed.

On January 26, 1904, fifteen, non-union miners at the Independence mine plummeted to their death when the cage broke free from its cable. Again, the W.F.M. was accused of foul play, despite having no access to the heavily guarded mine.

Before these mysterious incidents occurred, Peabody was preparing to recall the guardsmen who were deemed an unnecessary expense in the absence of violent protests. Instead, he was persuaded to declare martial law. General Bell in turn doubled down on his autocracy, announcing a suspension of the Bill of Rights.

Besides his state salary, Bell was being paid an additional $3,200 annually by the mine owners. When the payments fell behind, soldiers shot up the Vindicator shaft house in the night. The money came the next day. Bell was a loose cannon—a mad dog whose handlers had lost the leash. There seemed to be no line—legal, moral, or otherwise—that he would not cross to annihilate the union.

In June, a large group of non-union miners was waiting at the Independence train depot when the platform suddenly exploded beneath them. Thirteen men were killed and six were wounded. When the sheriff began an investigation, he was confronted by members of the Cripple Creek Mine Owner's Association (C.C.M.O.A.), who threatened to lynch him if he did not immediately resign.

This same group then organized a rally outside the W.F.M. union hall in Victor. When the city marshal attempted to break up the angry mob, he was fired on the spot by the anti-union mayor. In the streets, the situation was rapidly degrading into an all-out riot. C. C. Hamlin, secretary of the Mine Owner's Association, mounted an empty wagon and launched into a passionate tirade, urging the townspeople to oust the union. An irate striker produced a rifle and fired a shot at Hamlin, hitting another man instead. All hell broke loose as more people began shooting wildly into the crowd. Five men were cut down in the fray.

As townspeople scattered, the union miners retreated to their hall. Within minutes, the building was surrounded by militia troops demanding their surrender. When the miners refused, the soldiers opened fire. Bullets tore through the structure, shattering windows and striking four of the defending miners. Outmanned and outgunned, the union men could not hold out. They were soon captured and guardsmen ransacked the hall. The building still stands as it did on that fateful day, bullet holes and all.

That night, and in the days to come, union miners were rounded up and arrested in droves. They were tried personally by General Bell. Those who did not renounce the union were loaded onto a waiting train and dumped across the state line. Within a matter of days, all W.F.M. members had been deported from Cripple Creek.

Similarly, in Telluride, strikers at the Smuggler-Union and Tom Boy mines were arrested and expelled from the county. Bulkeley Wells, the new manager of the Smuggler-Union mine (replacing the murdered Arthur Collins), was appointed captain of his own state militia unit by Governor Peabody. Wells ordered the construction of a sentry post at the top of Imogene Pass to prevent union men from reentering Telluride. Snipers manned the stacked-stone redoubt, day and night, until 1908. The modest guardhouse was dubbed "Fort Peabody" in honor of the governor. It still stands today.

After the fall of the W.F.M., mining conditions in Colorado worsened. By 1910, the fatality rate for employed miners was three times the national average. The labor disputes would continue into the days of coal mining, ultimately culminating in the Colorado Coalfield Wars and the infamous Ludlow Massacre, but that shall be for another book.

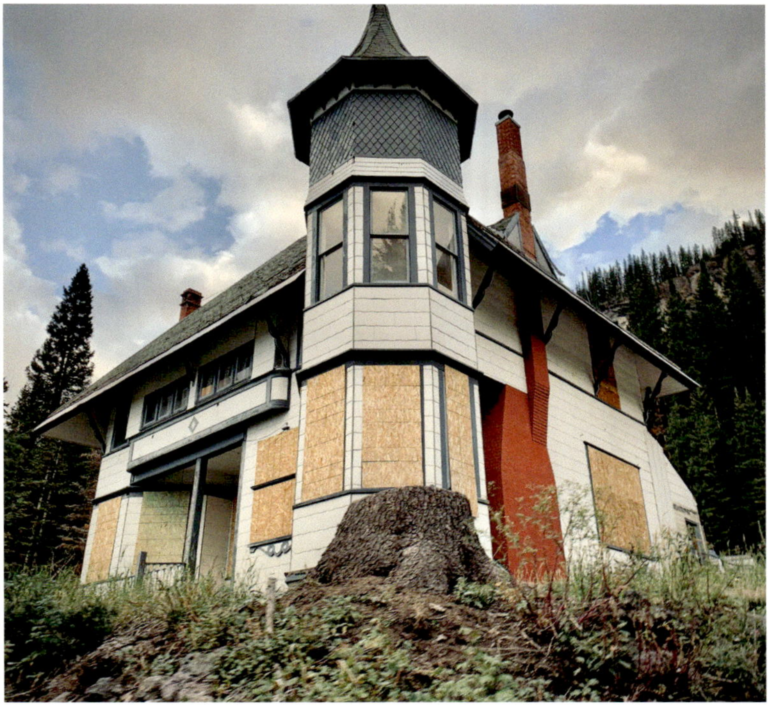

The stately mine manager's house at Camp Bird.

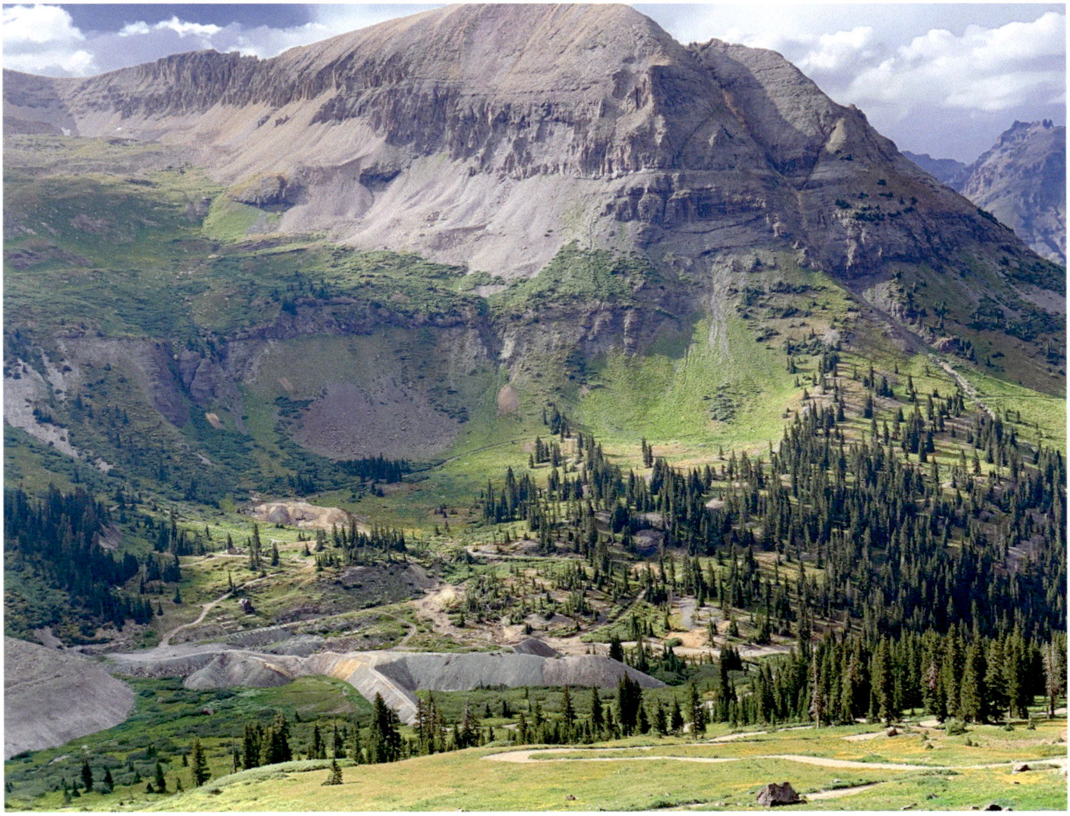

Huge tailings piles line Imogene Basin, remnants of the Upper Camp Bird operation.

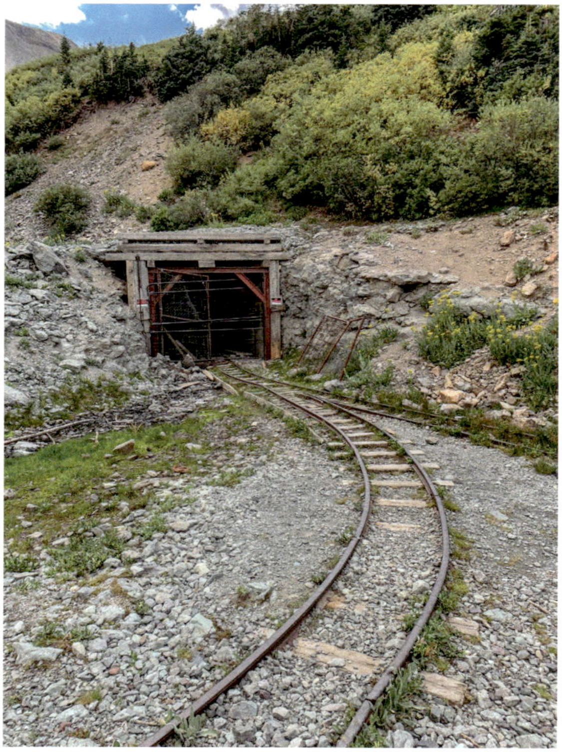

Left: Portal to Camp Bird No. 3 level.

Below: Ore cart tracks inside the Camp Bird mine.

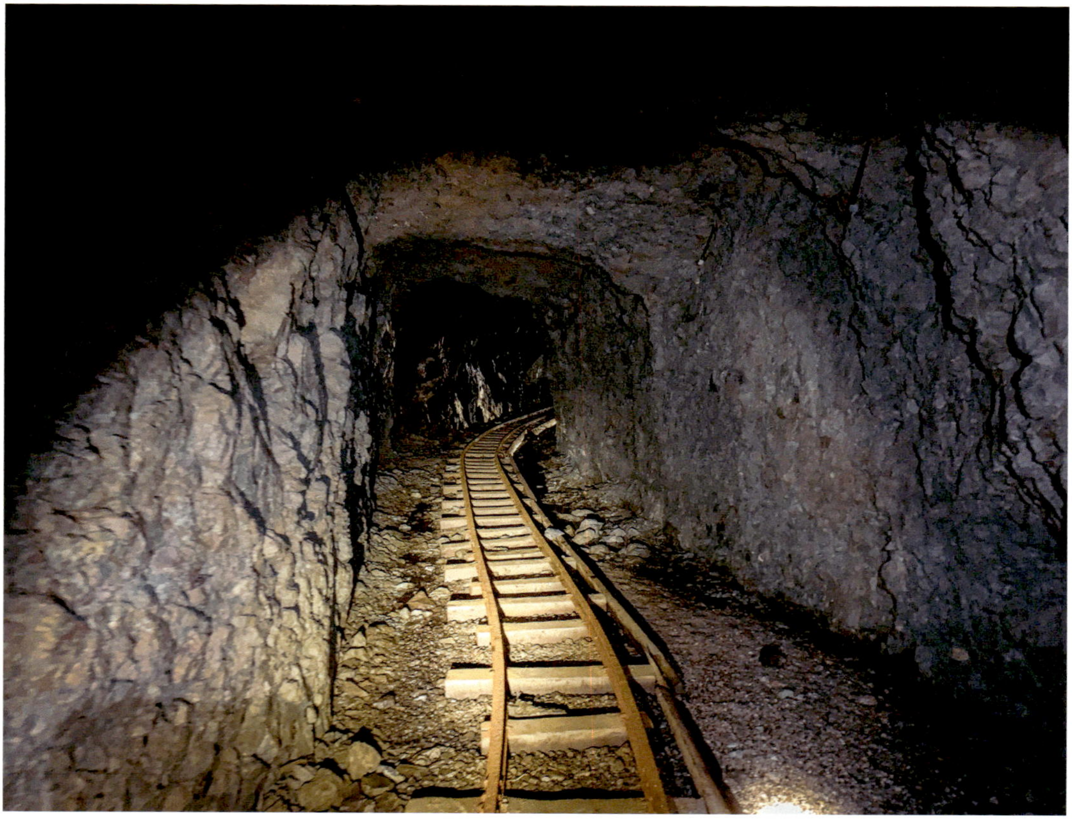

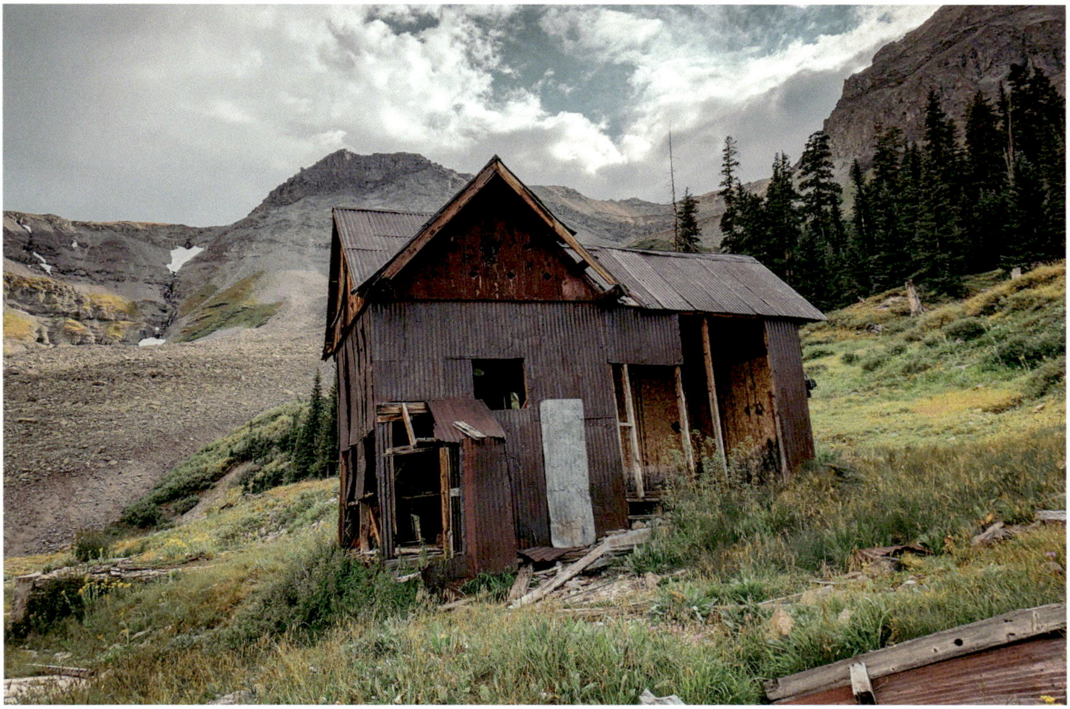

The only standing structure at Upper Camp Bird.

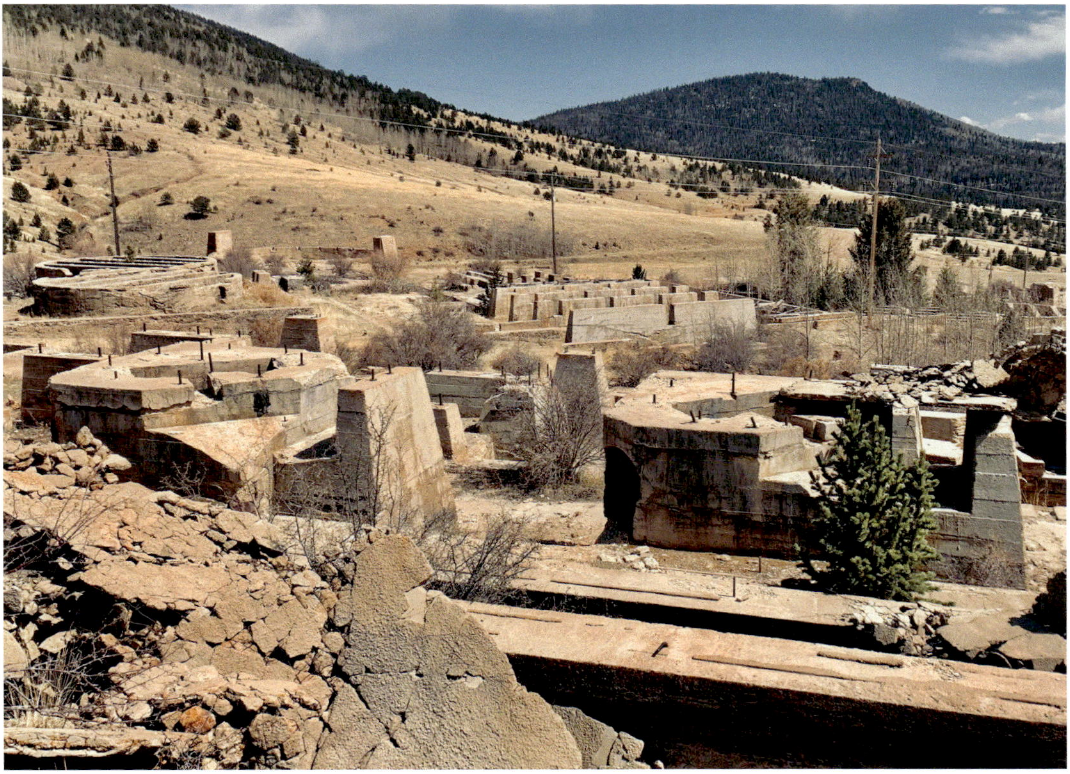

Castle-like ruins of the Independence Mill.

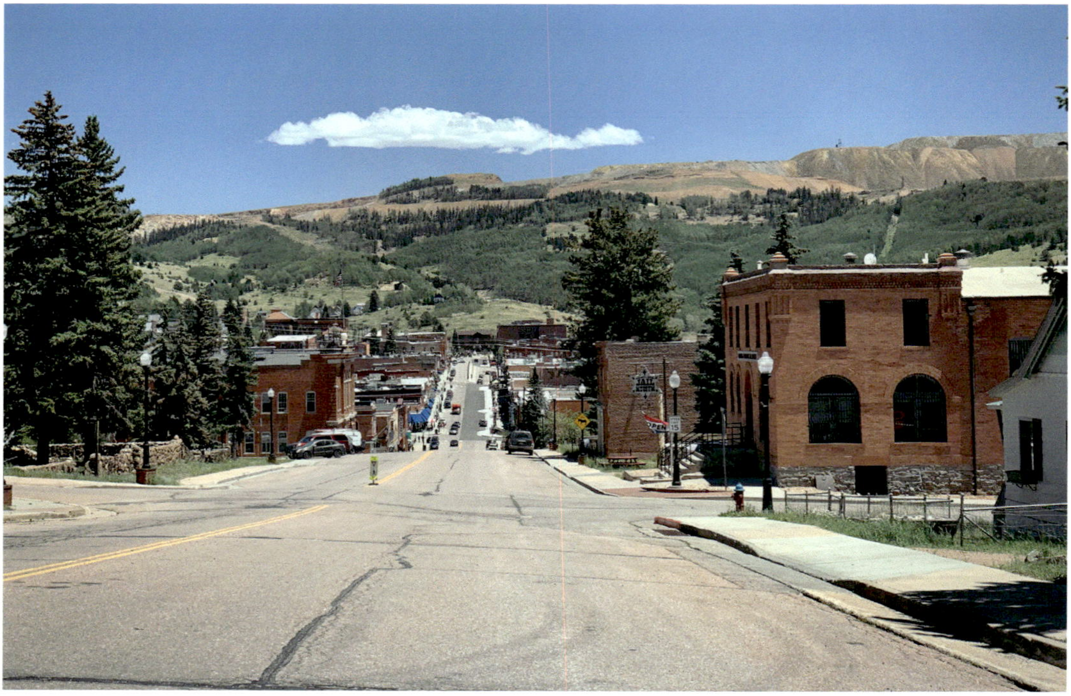

Cripple Creek, present day. The courthouse is the first building on the left. The old Teller County Jail sits on the corner, opposite.

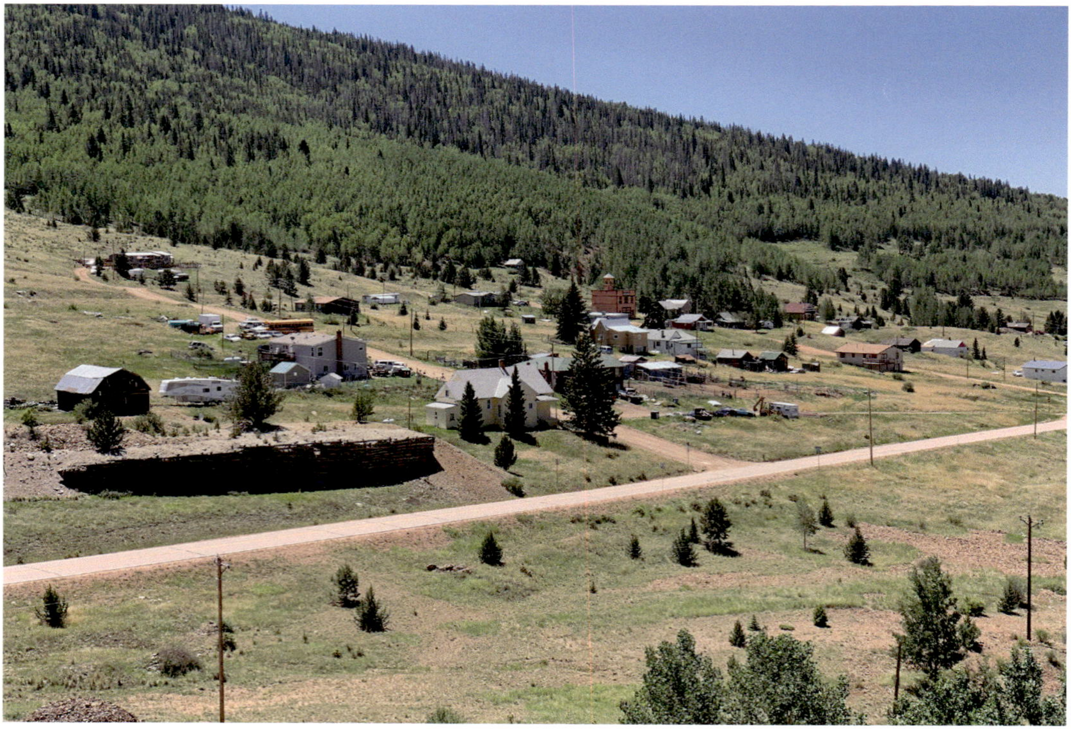

General Bell had a bullpen stockade built in the town of Goldfield (shown here) to imprison all those who opposed or spoke out against the guardsmen. Today, the town is nearly entirely abandoned.

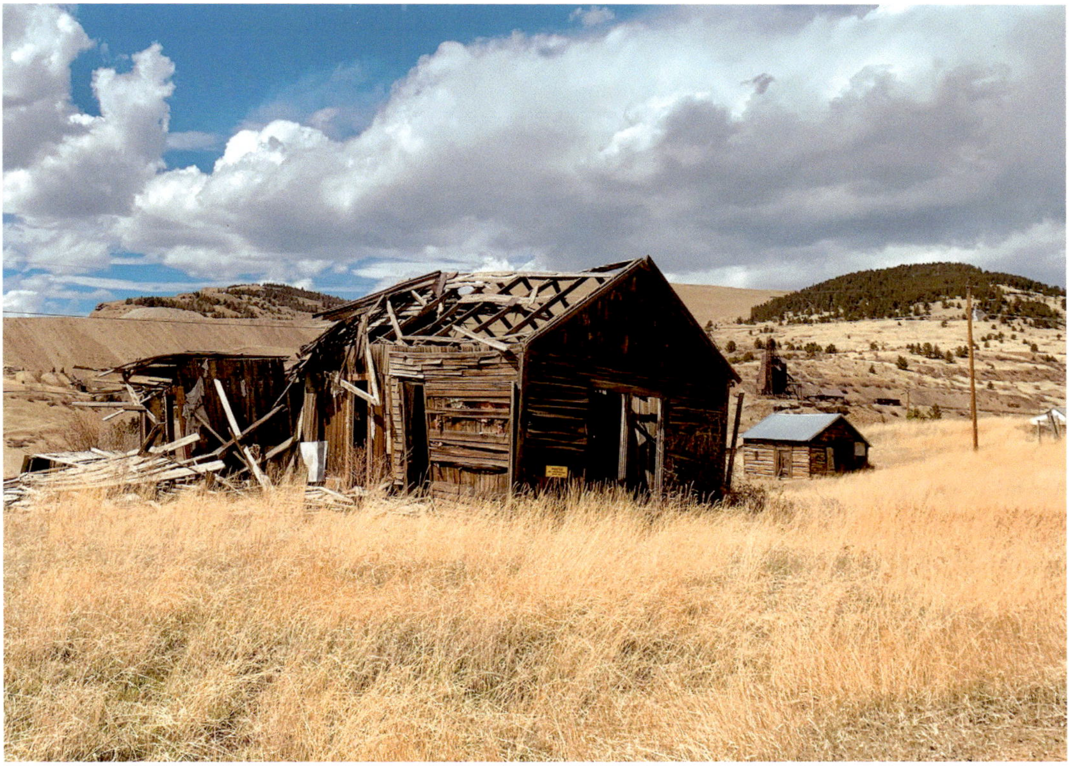

Above: A collapsing house in Goldfield. The Theresa mine can be seen on the far hill.

Right: The Goldfield City Hall, which doubled as the firehouse.

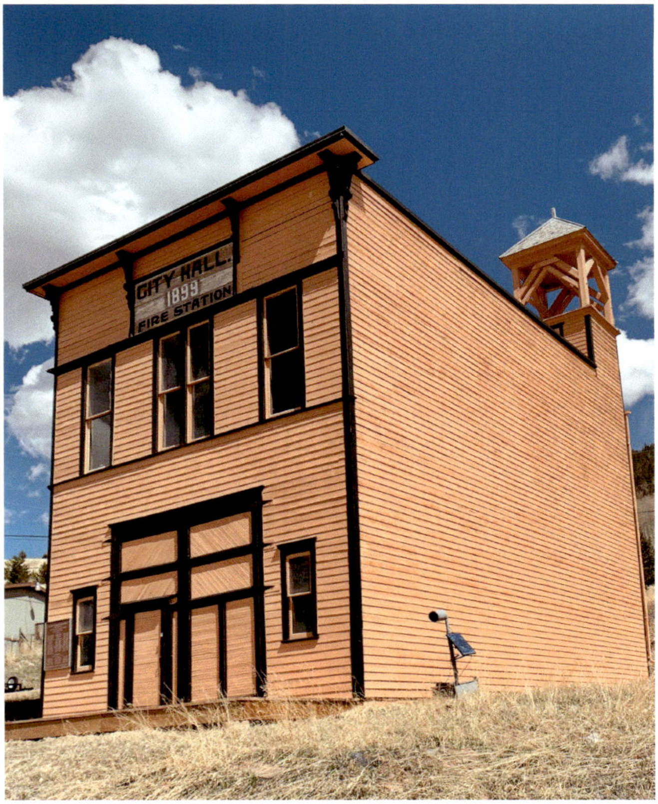

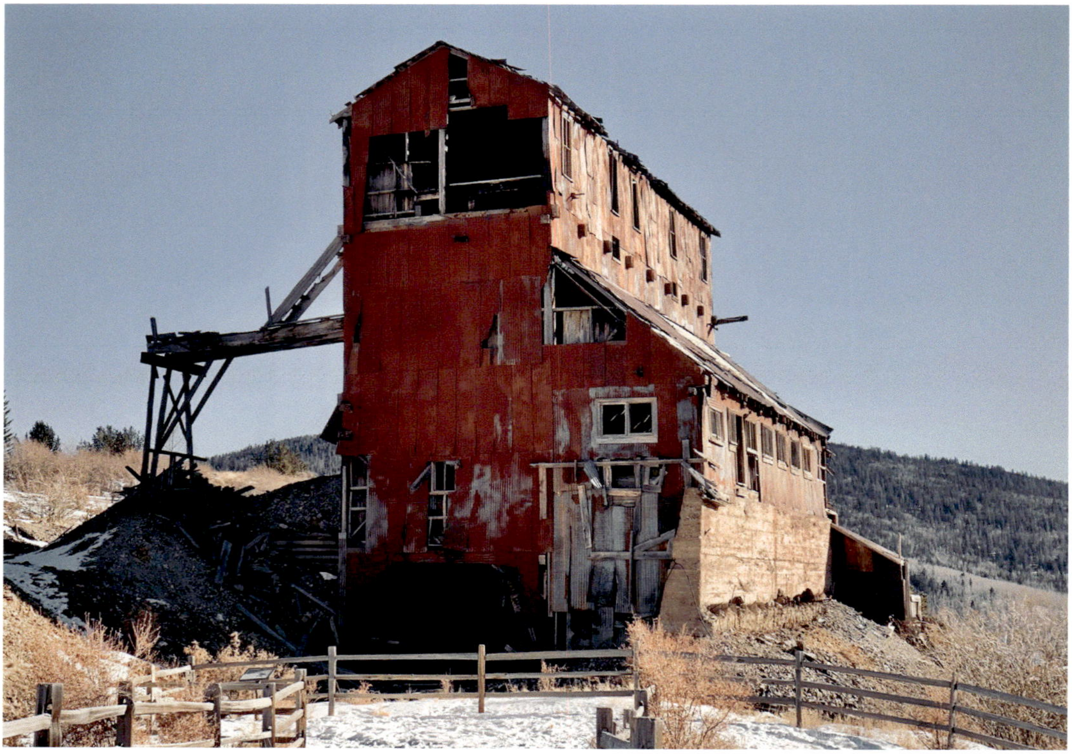

The ore house of the Vindicator mine. Being one of the largest operations in Cripple Creek, this mine became a clandestine battleground during the labor wars.

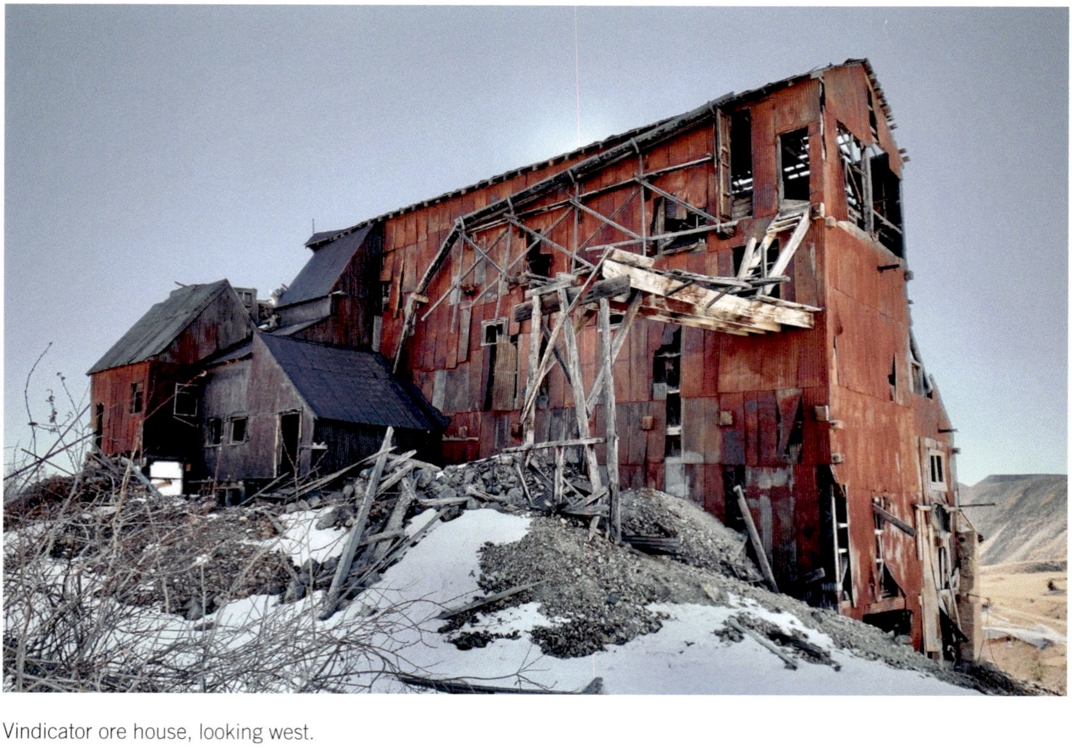

Vindicator ore house, looking west.

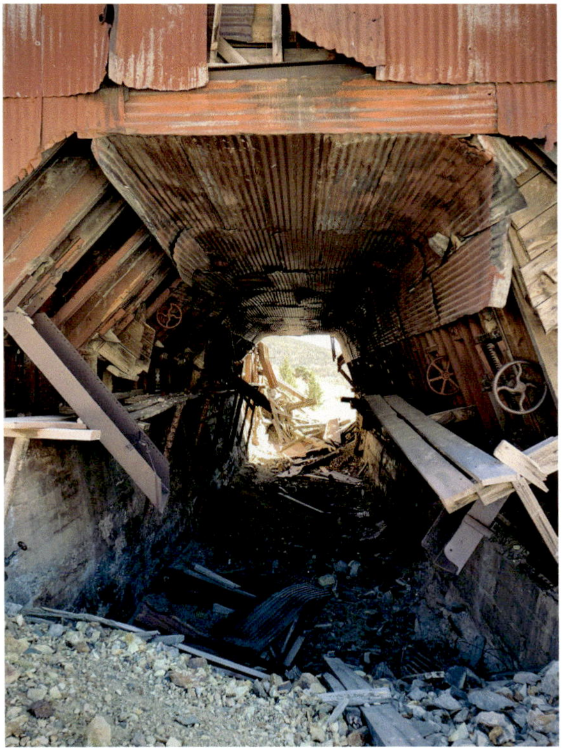

Right: A corridor beneath the Vindicator ore house allowed material to be dumped directly into waiting rail cars.

Below: A powder magazine near Battle Mountain. The explosives stored here were often pilfered for nefarious purposes during the Cripple Creek strike.

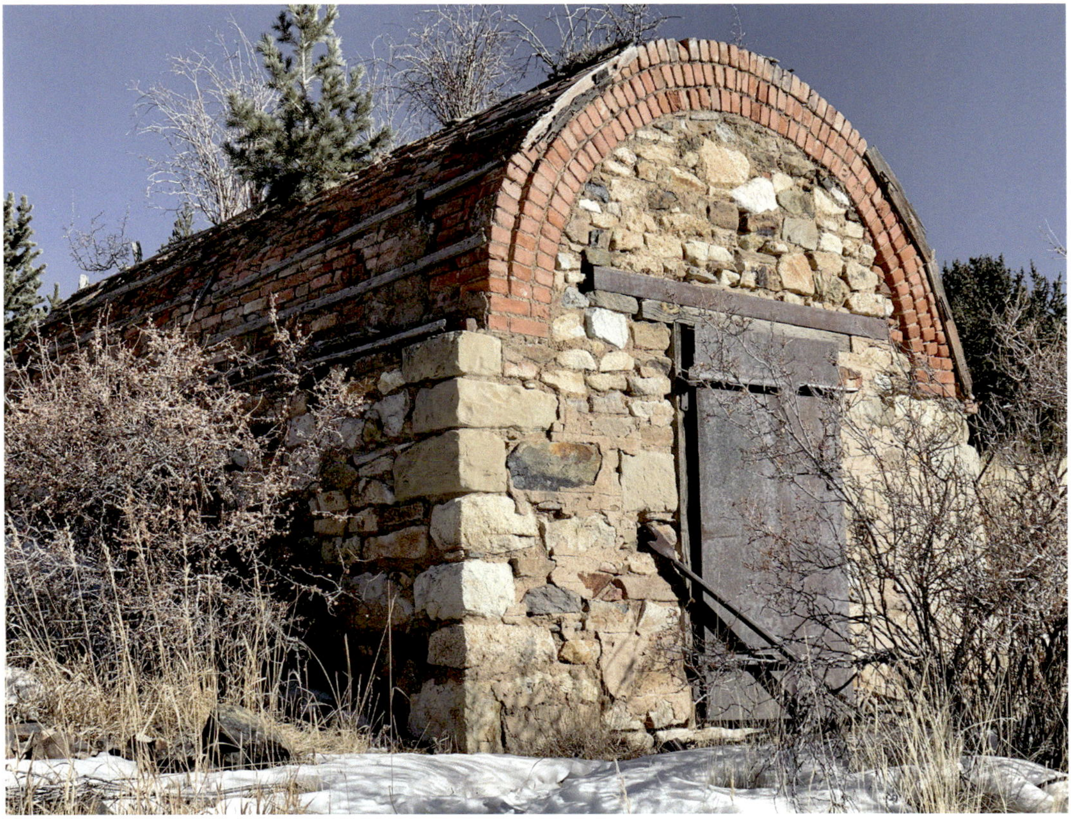

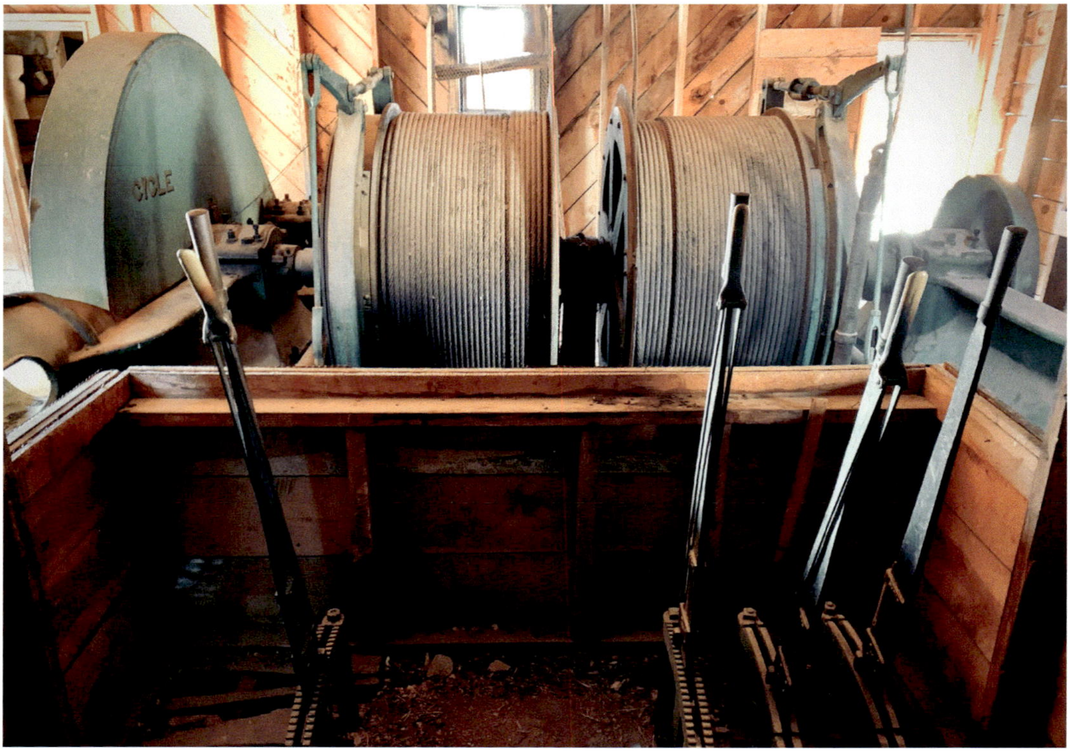
CYCLE

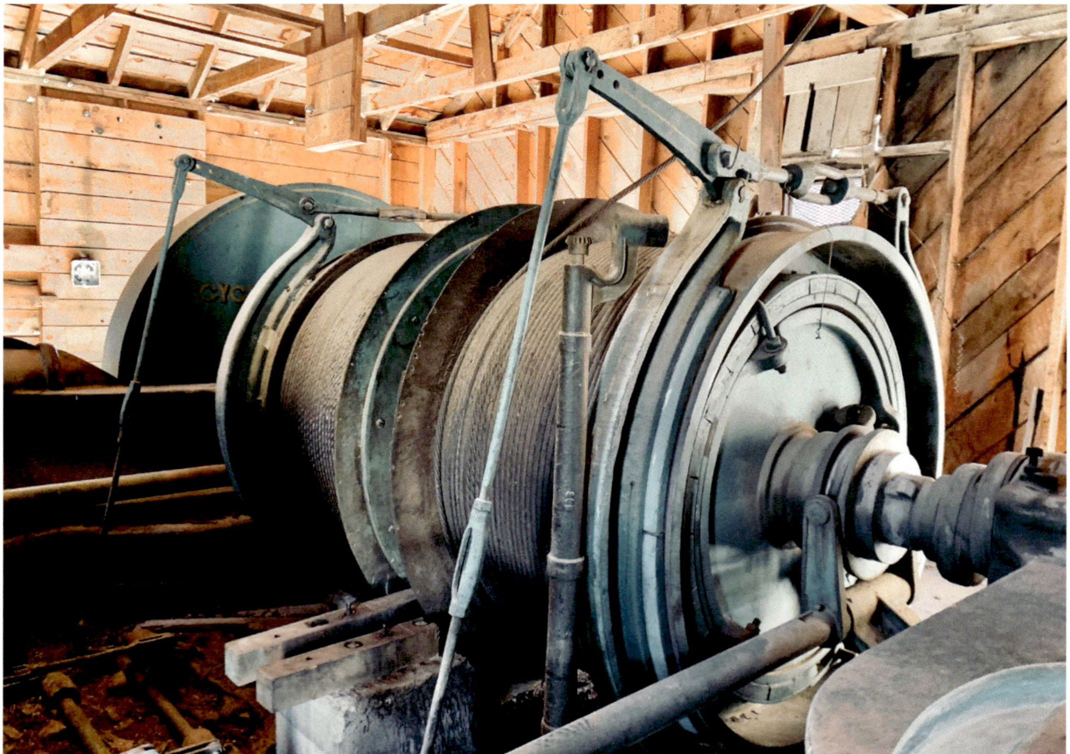

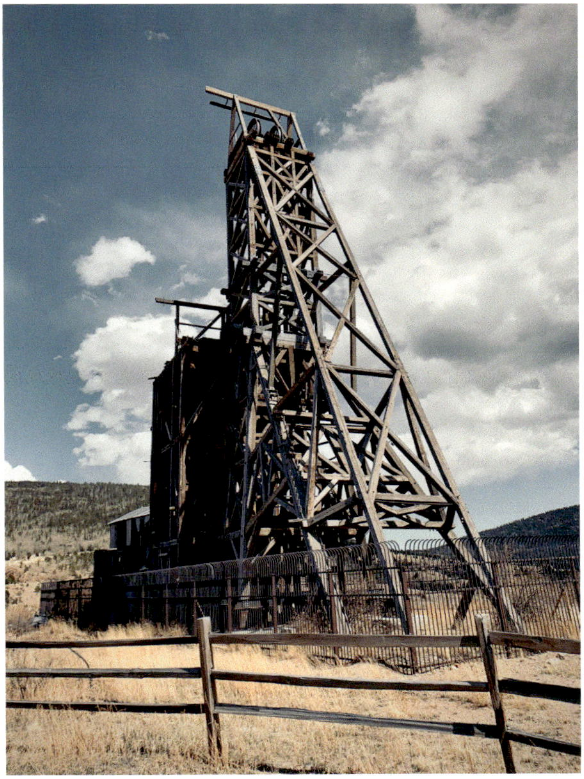

One man survived the incident at the Independence mine (shown here) by jumping into the timbers of the headframe just before the cage fell. Remnants of his coworkers were found scattered across multiple levels of the 1,500-foot-deep shaft.

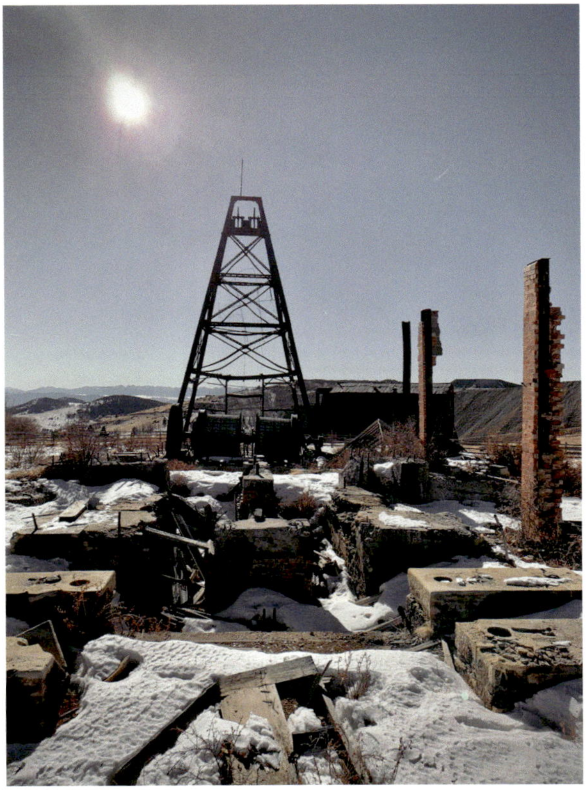

The headframe and ruins of the shaft house at the Vindicator mine.

Opposite above: Hoist controls at the Theresa mine, similar to those at the Independence mine. The engineer on duty at the time of the accident claimed that the brakes were jammed, causing the cage full of miners to be pulled into the sheave wheel where it broke free.

Opposite below: Hoists like this Wellman-Seaver-Morgan double-drum were normally equipped with backup disk brakes. Investigators at the Independence mine discovered that this system had been detached.

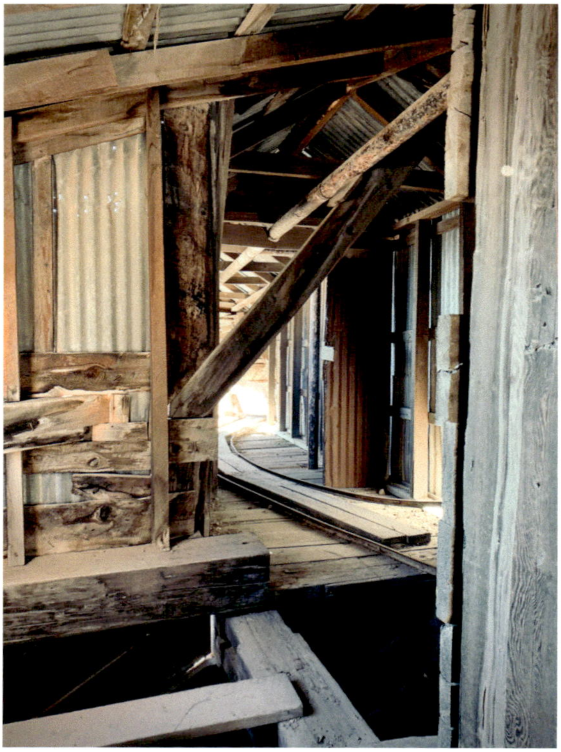

Left: Interior of the Vindicator ore house.

Below: The now-defunct Midland Terminal Railroad Depot in Victor.

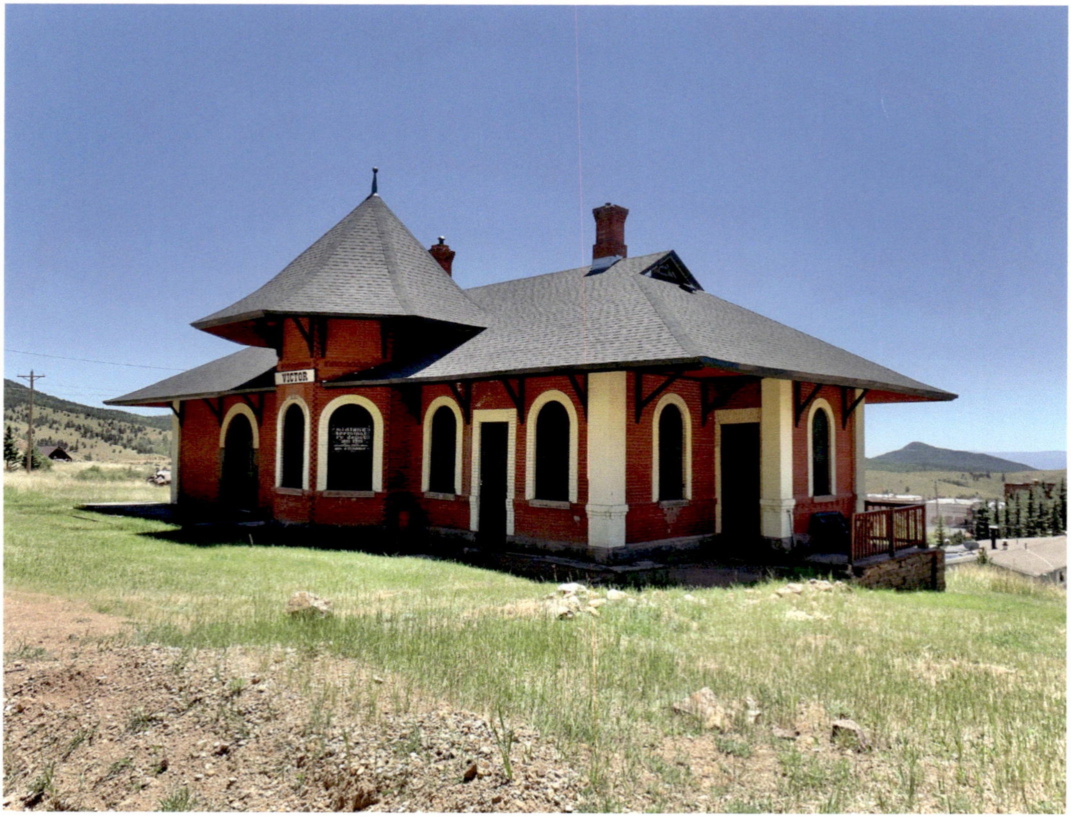

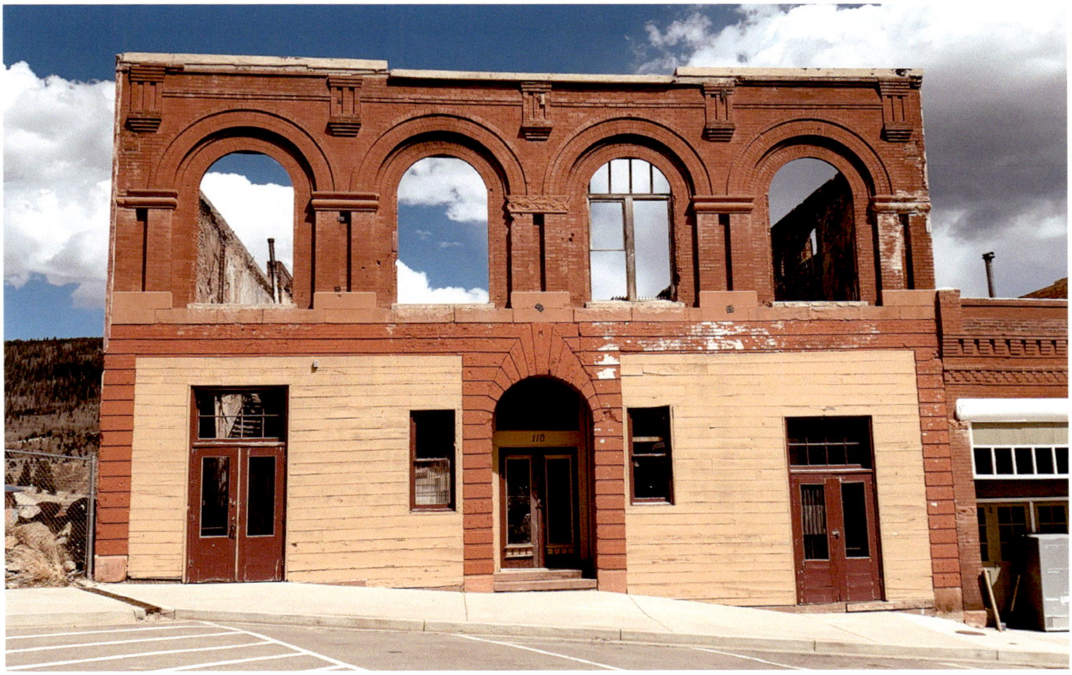

The Western Federation of Miners union hall in Victor. The building was ransacked by militiamen following a violent riot in the streets.

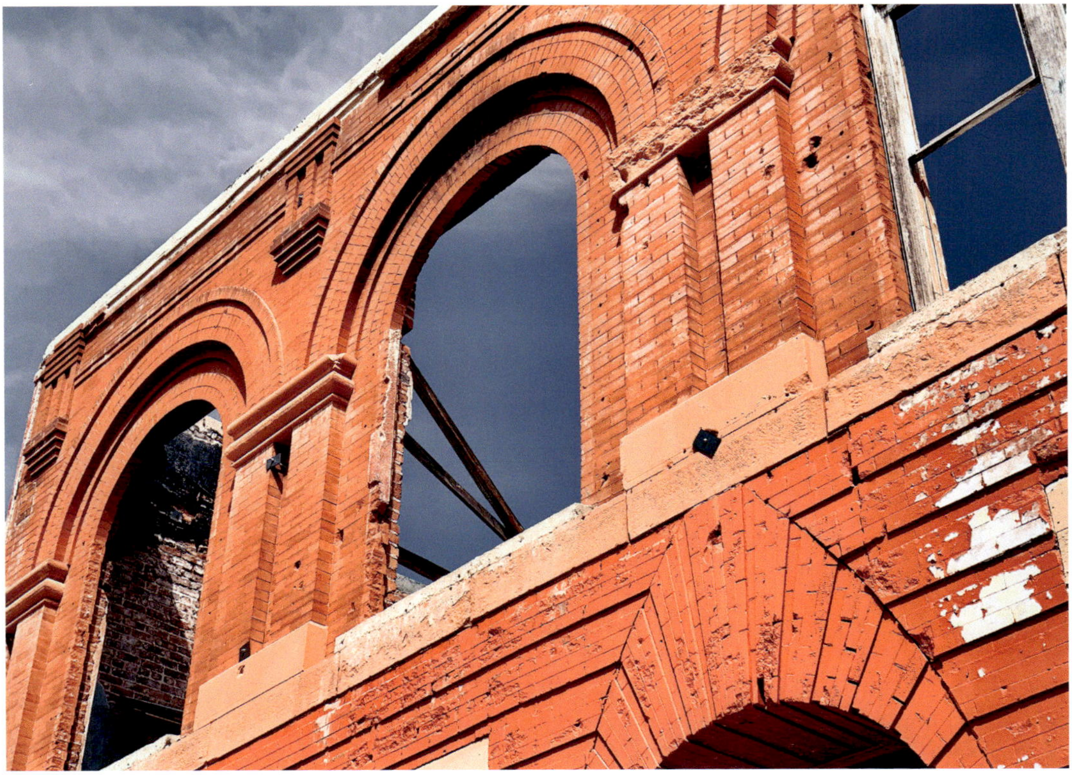

Bullet holes from the final battle can still be seen in the masonry of the W.F.M. hall.

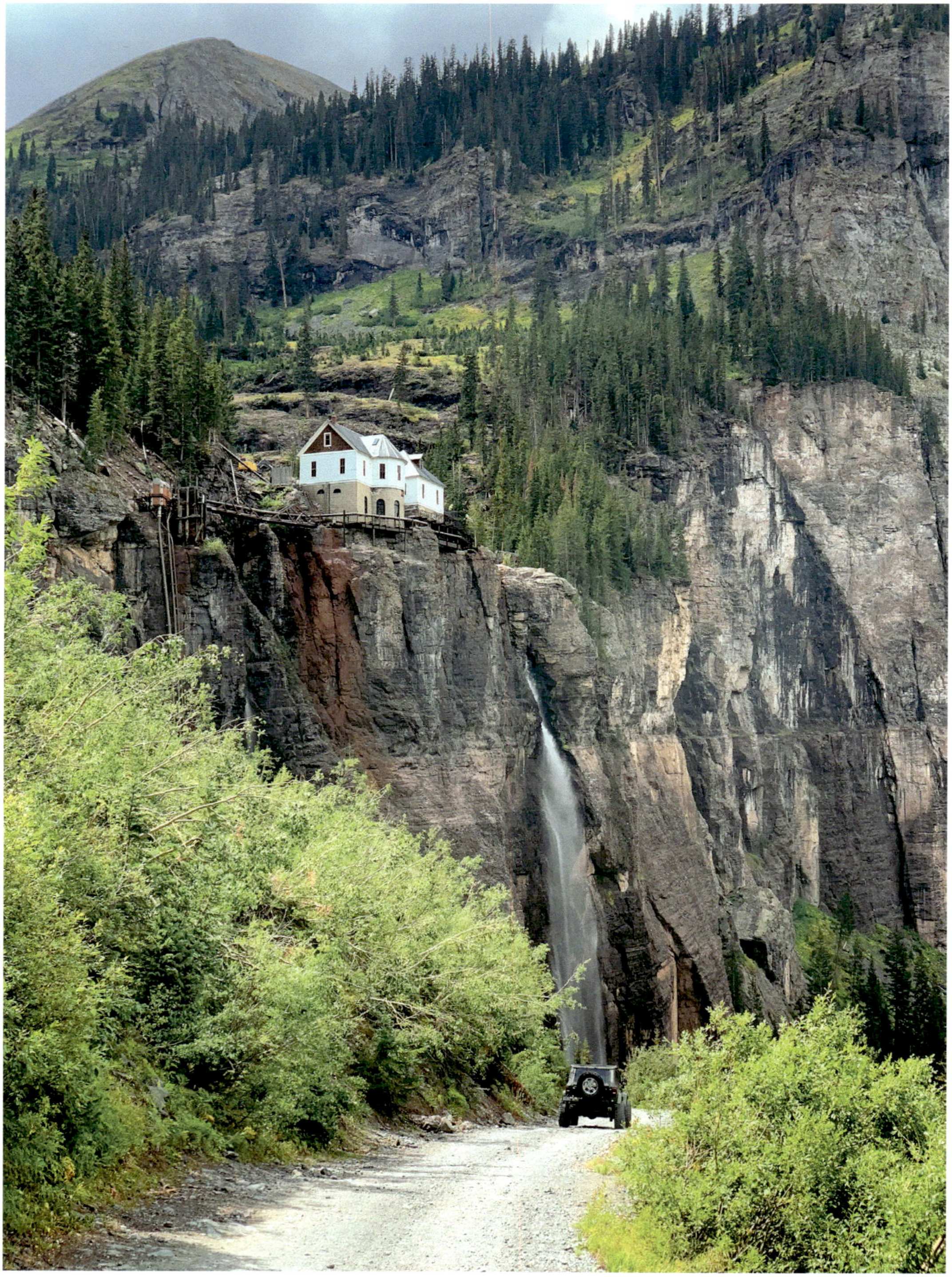

The Smuggler-Union Hydroelectric Power Plant was built in 1907 by mine manager Buckely Wells to provide power for industrial operations. Wells used the plant as a summer home until 1920.

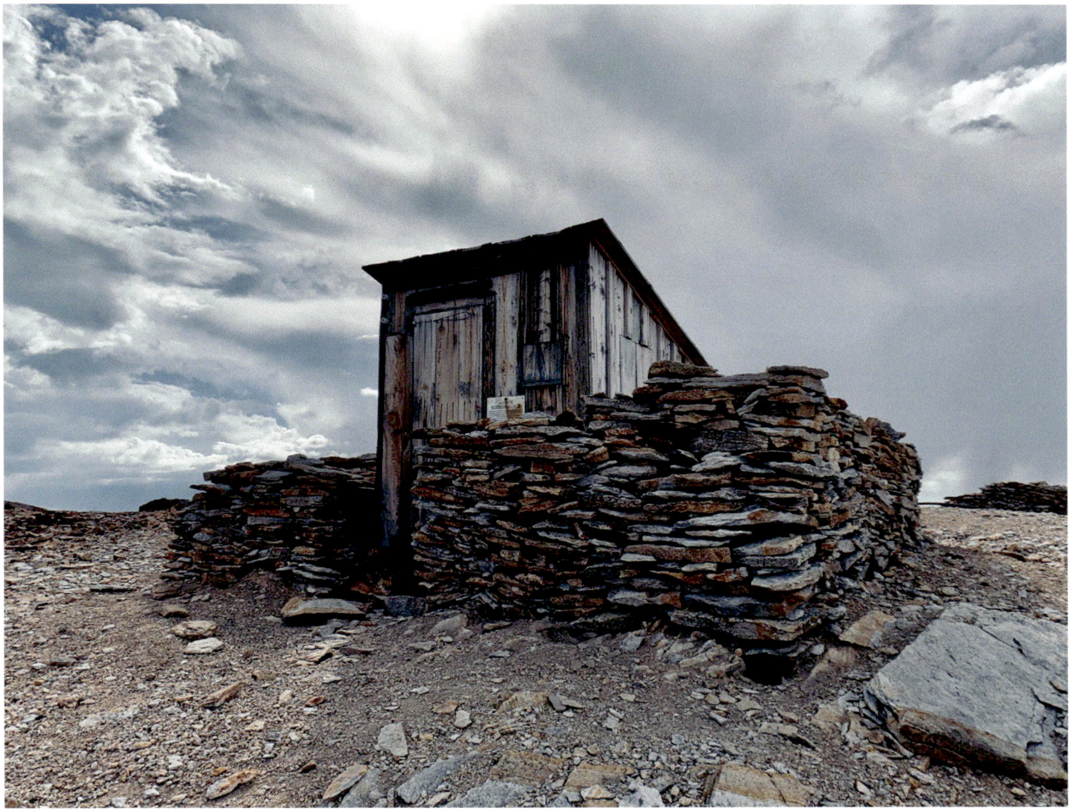

"Fort Peabody" was little more than a wooden shack with stone walls built around it. The structure was stabilized in 2010.

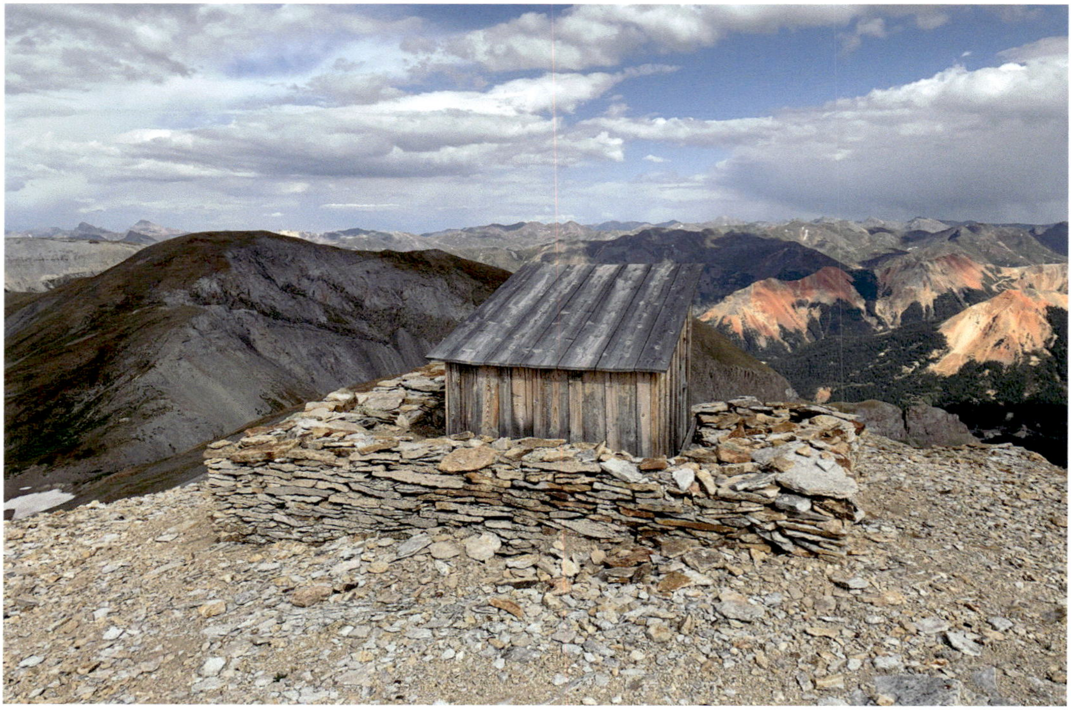

From their perch atop the hill, militiamen had a spectacular vantage point from which to watch the pass. Red Mountain is in the background.

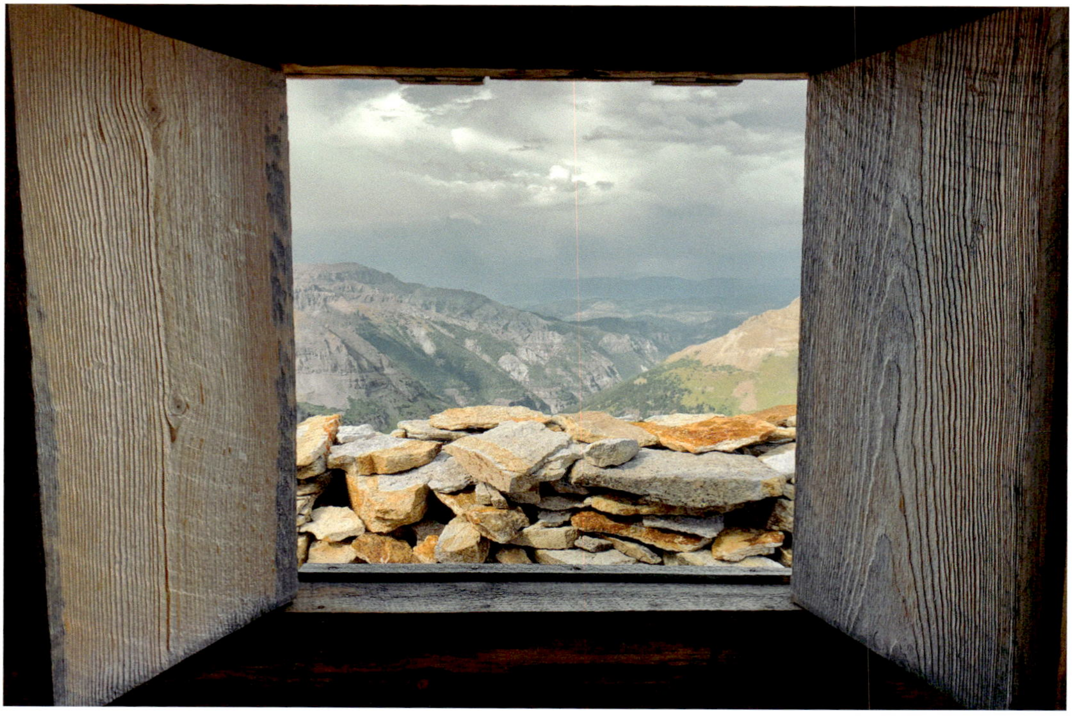

Some historical texts make mention of a Colt machine gun being installed at the guard post, and the structure is often referred to as Fort Peabody's machine gun nest.

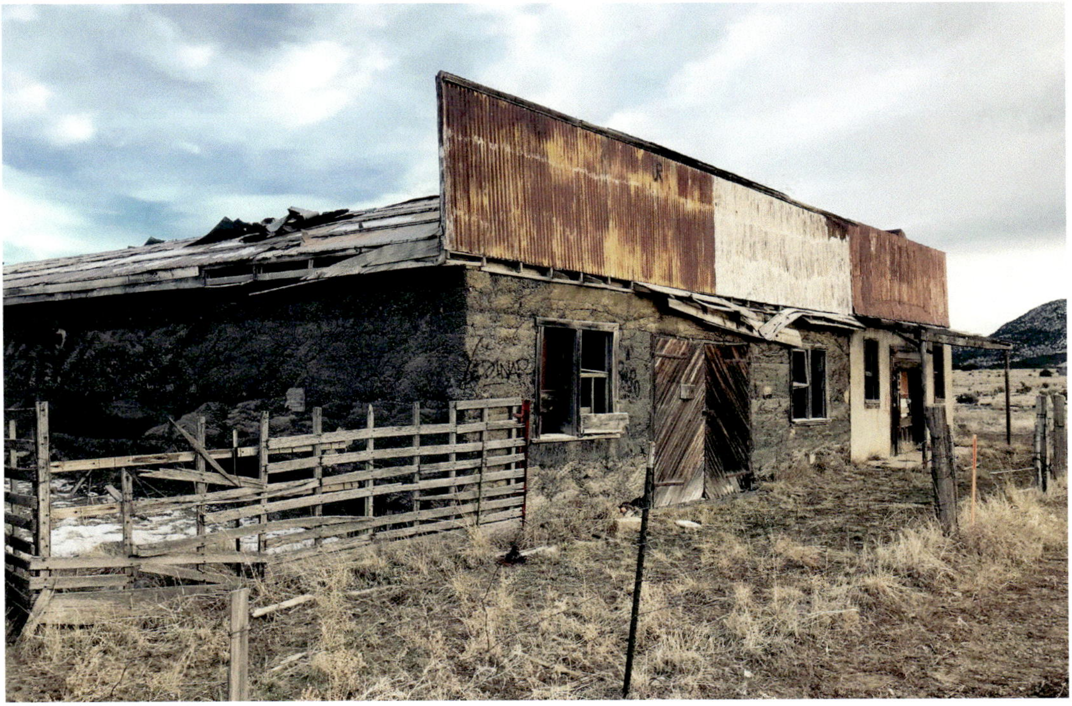

A few, flat-front buildings still line the streets of Ludlow. In 1914, the coal town was the scene of a major labor strike, which ended with the massacre of at least fifteen women and children. Some sources claim fifty-five.

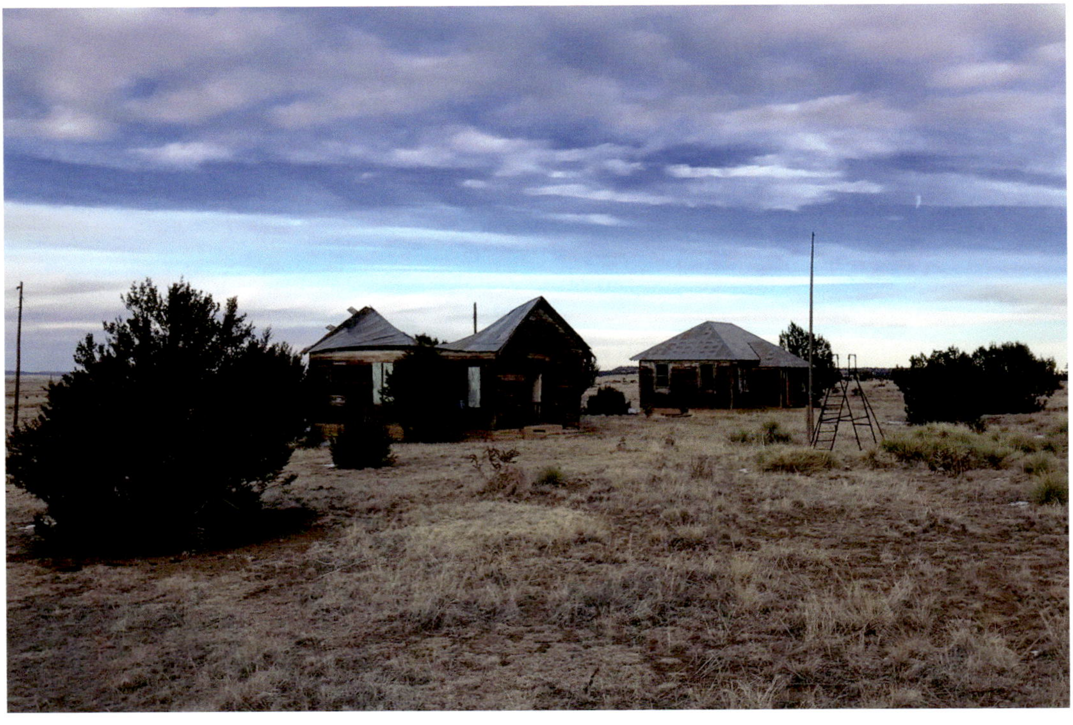

A pair of schoolhouses sit at the Ludlow townsite. The battle that took place here sparked a ten-day war between miners all across Southern Colorado and the state national guard. Federal troops had to be deployed to disarm both sides.

6

WHAT REMAINS

World War One signaled the end of an era for Colorado. Gold prices had dropped significantly and would remain low until the Great Depression. As men left to fight overseas, many mines and settlements were abandoned. By then, the edges of the map had all been filled in. The glory days of prospecting uncharted ranges were over—the Wild West had been tamed.

Behind them, the industrious pioneers of Colorado left a legacy of timber and iron. Lifeless towns list and lean in the shadows of disemboweled mountains. Palatial mills from which pure gold once poured out to the drum of beating stamps now lay quiet, save for the occasional clang of tin panels in the wind. Beneath it all is a dead honeycomb of forgotten passages—a veritable world, isolated from the entropic onslaught of time. These are the spoils of the modern adventurer.

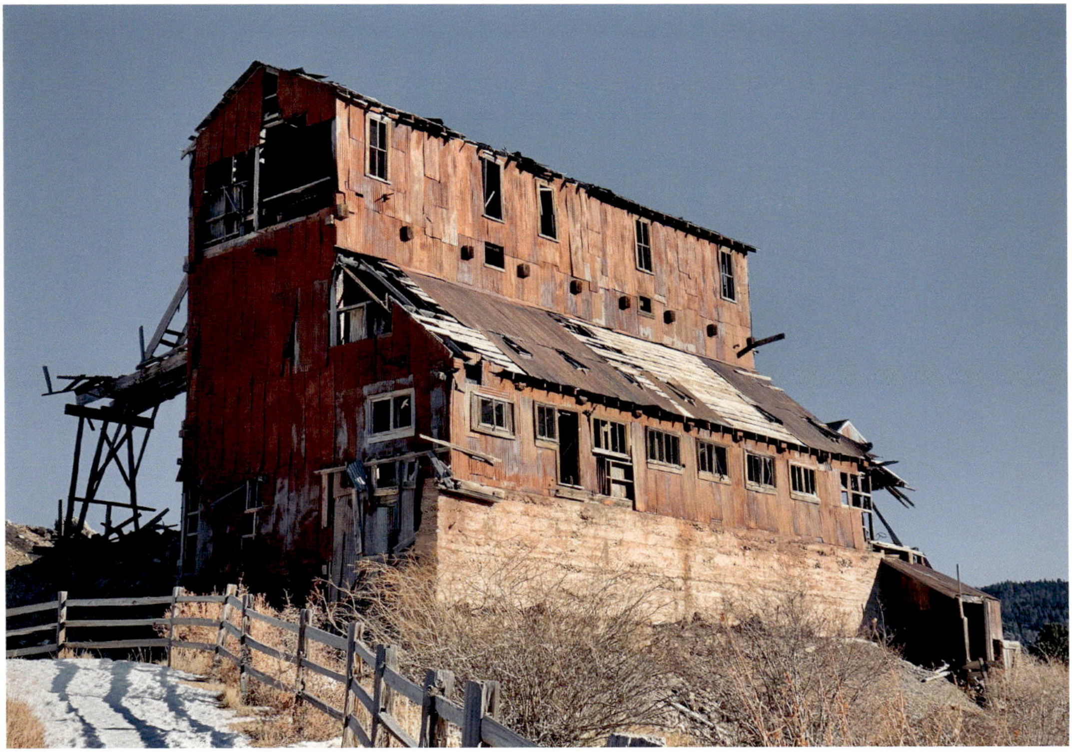

Ore house at the Vindicator mine in Cripple Creek.

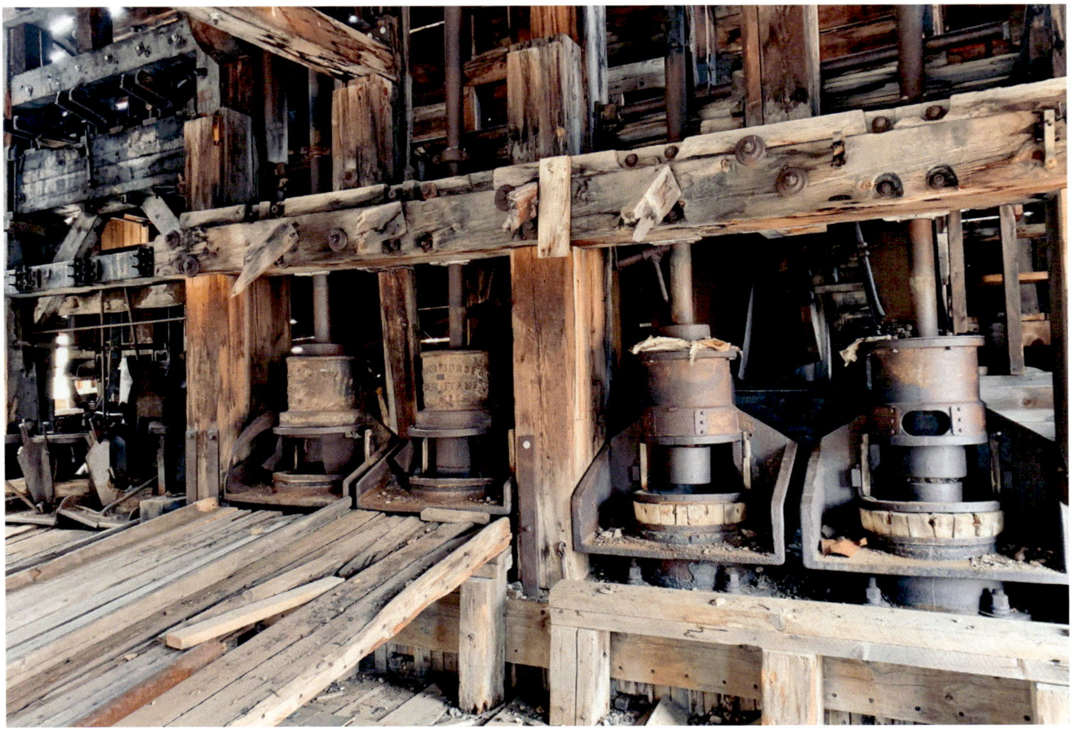

Stamp batteries at the Sound Democrat Mill.

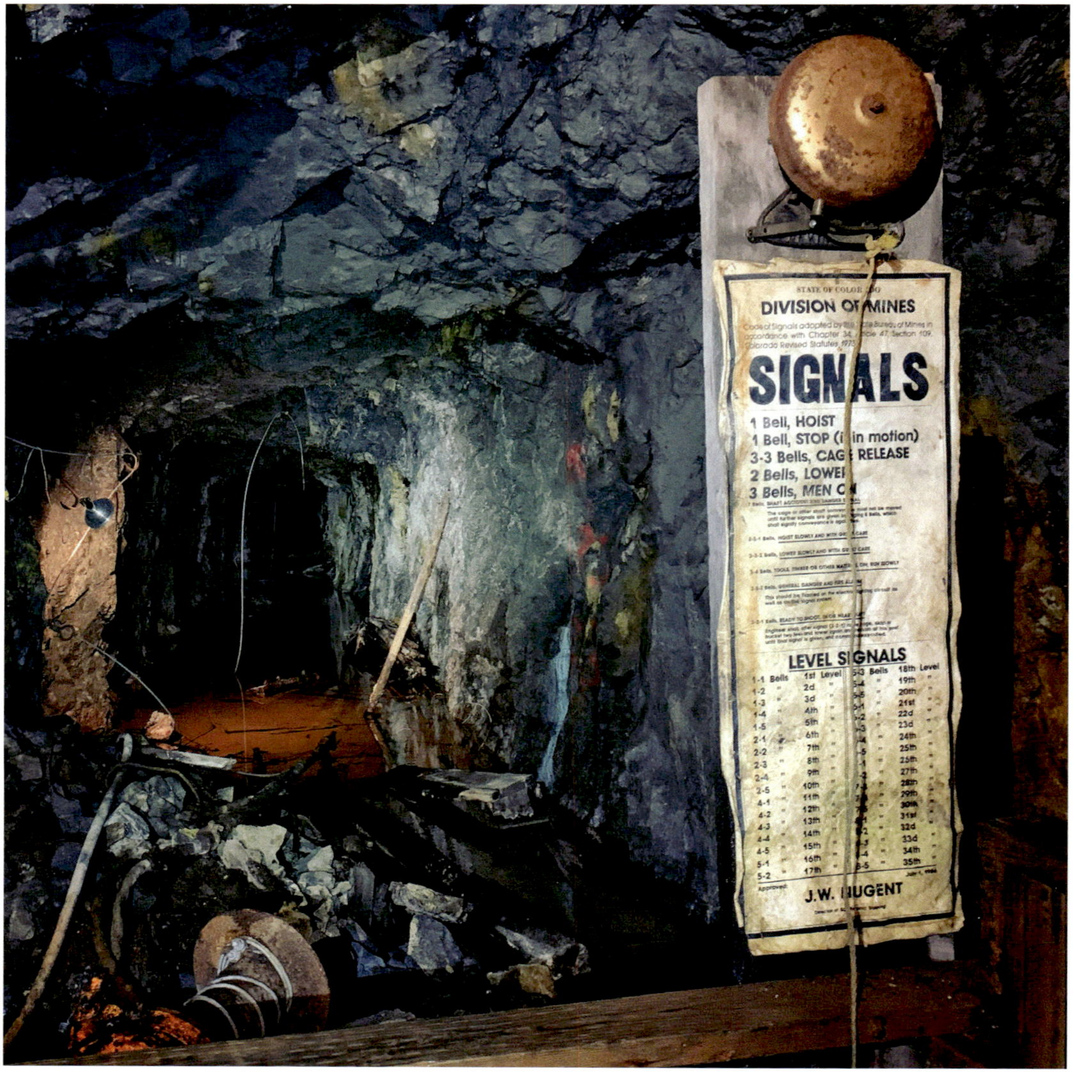

A hoist signal chart inside the Old Hundred mine.

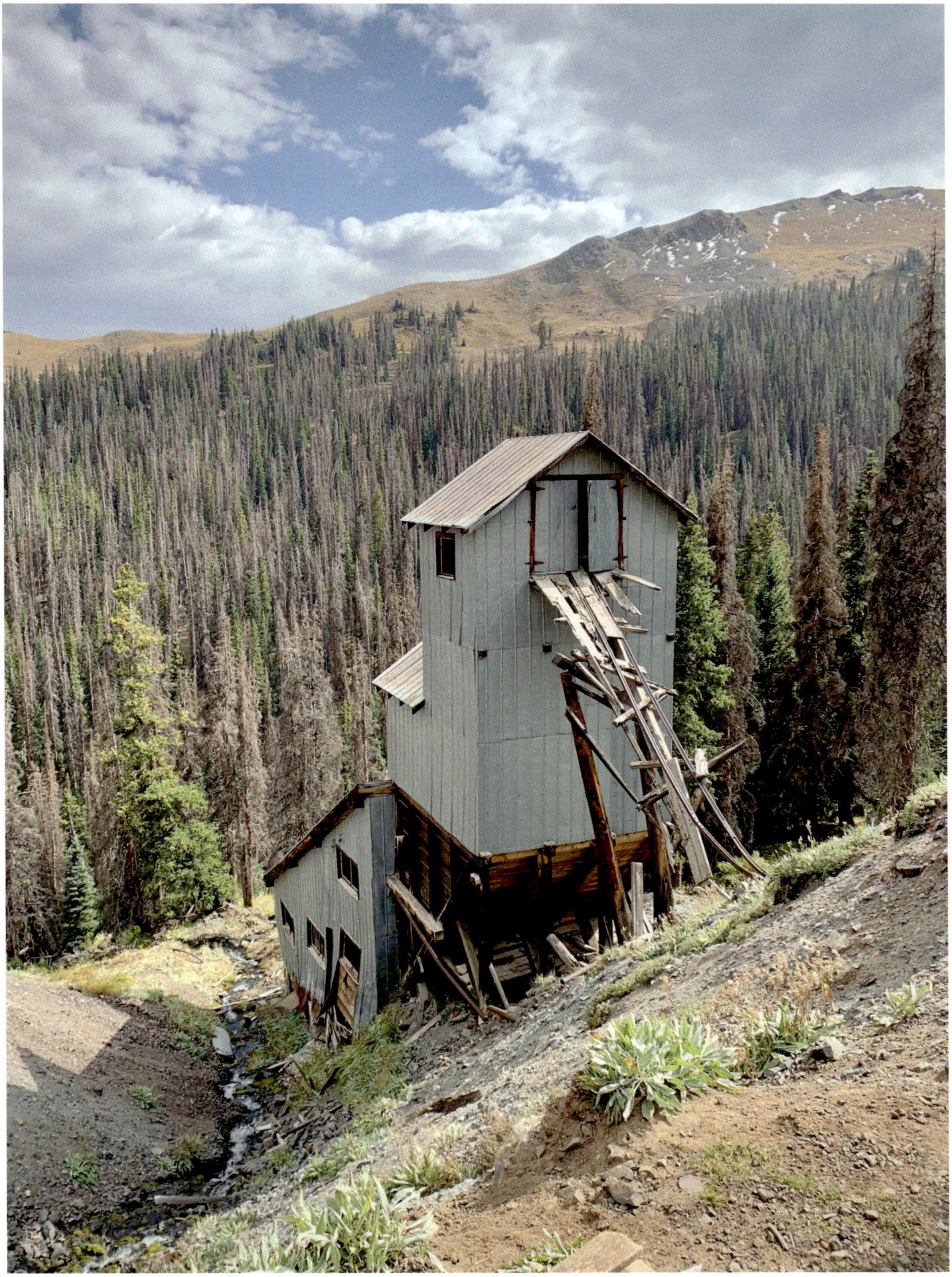

A small, stamp mill at the Treasure Mountain mine.

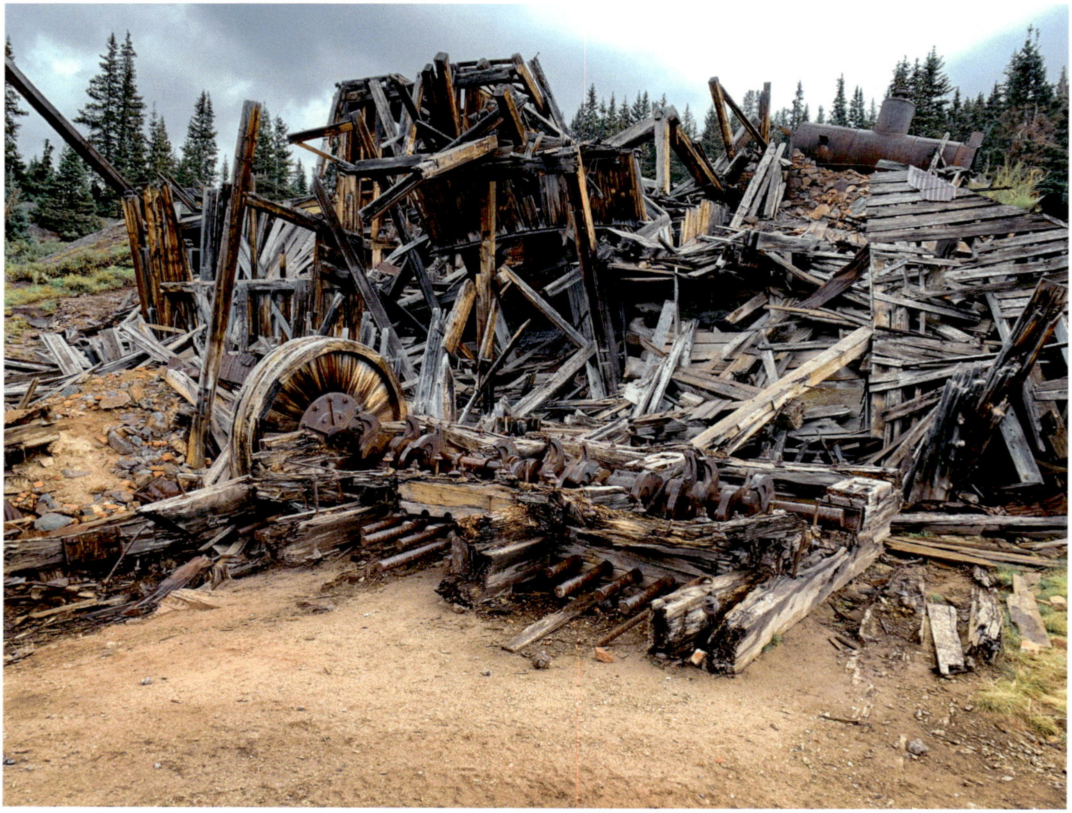

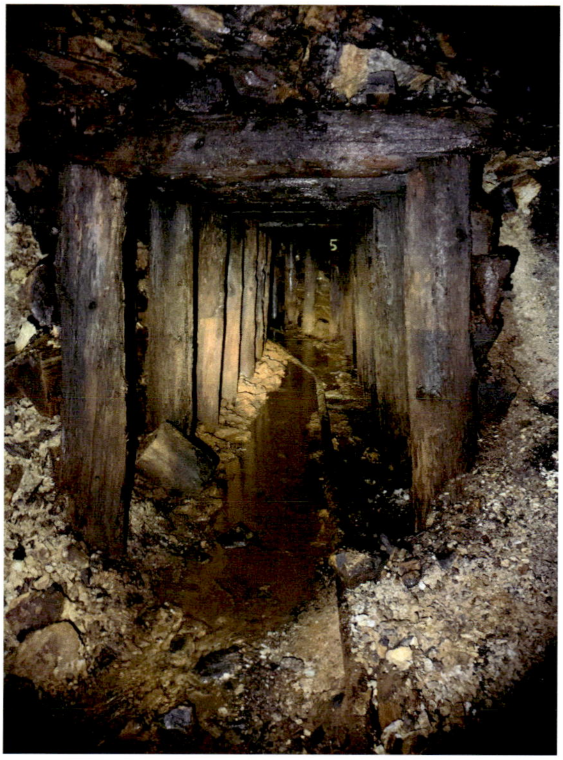

Above: Time has taken its toll on this mill at Mineral Point.

Left: Inside an abandoned drift in Sidney Basin. The name of the mine is unknown.